10-24-66

University of Cambridge
Department of Applied Economics
OCCASIONAL PAPERS 10

GROWTH RATE TABLES

University of Cambridge

Department of Applied Economics

Occasional Papers

GROWTH RATE TABLES

by H. T. BURLEY

Research Officer
Department of Applied Economics
Cambridge

CAMBRIDGE
AT THE UNIVERSITY PRESS
1966

PUBLISHED BY   OCT 2 4 '66

THE SYNDICS OF THE CAMBRIDGE UNIVERSITY PRESS

Bentley House, 200 Euston Road, London N. W. 1

American Branch: 32 East 57th Street, New York, N. Y. 10022

West African Office: P. M. B. 5181, Ibadan, Nigeria

©   DEPARTMENT OF APPLIED ECONOMICS
UNIVERSITY OF CAMBRIDGE
1966

 PRODUCED BY Uneoprint
set on electric keyboards
photo-reproduced and printed offset

at The Gresham Press
UNWIN BROTHERS LIMITED
Old Woking   Surrey   England

Contents

1449342

Preface

The purpose of these Growth Tables is to provide the answer to such questions as: at what rate of growth per annum must an economy expand in order to grow 25 per cent in six years? Normal compound interest tables are not adapted to supply easy answers to questions such as this, since they specify given rates of growth per year (or other period) and indicate what the final amount will be after a certain number of years. To answer this question one would therefore have to find the two rates which gave final amounts after six years, one rather above 125 and one rather below 125, and then interpolate between these two rates to get the exact answer. The tables in this publication, on the other hand, provide a rate of growth correct to two decimal places for time-spans up to 200 periods and final amounts up to 5,000 per cent of the initial amount. This layout should make the tables of interest to a wide range of users.

Two sets of tables are included. Table 1 in effect rearranges the usual tables of compound interest, where interest is added to the amount at the end of each year or period. Table 2 tabulates instantaneous growth rates, where interest or growth is accrued at the annual rate appearing in the table, but is added to the amount at infinitely small intervals of time.

These computations were performed on TITAN, the electronic computer at the University Mathematical Laboratory, Cambridge, by kind permission of its director, Professor M. V. Wilkes. Mrs Valerie Lea assisted with program preparation and the listing of output. The printing plates were prepared by photographical process, thus avoiding typographical errors.

The author wishes to express his gratitude for their collaboration to W. B. Reddaway, Director of the Department of Applied Economics, Cambridge, and Aubrey Silberston.

University of Cambridge
Department of Applied Economics   H. T. B.

March 1966

Introduction: How to Use the Tables

In these tables the rate of growth required is read from the element in the table at the row corresponding to the final amount and in the column appropriate to the time-span. The final amount in the tables is based on an initial amount of 100 per cent and thus a total growth of 50 per cent would be represented by a final amount of 150. The time-span is the number of periods over which the growth rate of r per cent per period has applied.

Of course the time-span need not necessarily be a number of <u>years</u>, though the year is the commonest unit to use in considering rates of growth. Strictly, the "period" to use is the interval of time which the element of growth is compounded with the existing amount, as a basis for calculating the amount of growth that will take place in the next period. In compound interest work, for example, if the interest is added to the principal at the end of each half-year, then the period to use is a half-year even though the rate of interest is generally expressed as (for example) 6 per cent per annum. If, in fact, 3 per cent is added to the principal at the end of each half-year (and the interest for the next half-year is calculated as 3 per cent of 103, rather than 100), then the time span over which growth is being considered should be (say) 20 half years rather than 10 years, and the appropriate table to be used would be that for 20 periods and a growth rate of 3 per cent.

If the user wishes to use these tables for a final amount or period which is not exactly specified in the tables, then he would have to consult the two adjacent elements in the table closest to the final amount or period he requires and interpolate between them for the particular growth rate he requires.

The tables can also be used as ordinary compound interest tables to find (say) the final amount corresponding to a growth rate of 5 per cent and a period of 20 years. In this case one would scan down the 20 periods column of the table until one found an interest rate at or near 5 per cent. The final amount can then be read, or interpolated, from the left-hand side (or final amount) of this row of the table.

Table 1. Rates of growth (compounding each period)

In the body of this table the annual rates of growth appropriate to the "final amount" in the left hand column, and the number of periods (in the top row) are presented correct to two decimal places. The growth rates are themselves percentages. Where A is the final amount to which an initial quantity of 100 would have grown to in t periods, the growth rate r satisfies the following equation:-

$$A = 100 \left(1 + \frac{r}{100}\right)^t$$

This is, in effect, a rearrangement of the usual table of compound interest, where growth at the rate of r per period is compounded each period. If, on the other hand, the growth is continuous (being compounded at every instant of time) or t is very large then Table 2 would be appropriate.

Examples of use of the Table

1.   What is the average annual rate of growth of a national income which doubles in 25 years?

These tables are based on original amount of 100. An increase of 100% yields a final amount of 200, which, at 25 periods in Table 1 shows a rate of growth of 2.81% per annum.

2.   If the population of a certain city grows at an average rate of 1.65% per annum, by what percentage will its population increase in 17 years?

In Table 1 we scan down the 17 years column until we find in the body of the table a growth rate of 1.65%. This corresponds to 132 in the Final Amount column, representing a 32% increase over the 17 years.

3.   If the rate of growth referred to in example 2 were 1.680% per year, by what percentage would the population of the city increase in 17 years?

The column in the table corresponding to 17 periods show us an annual rate of 1.65% would yield a final amount of 132 after 17 years, and an annual rate of 1.69% would yield a final amount of 133 after 17 years. To obtain the final amount corresponding to the 1.68% growth rate we have to interpolate three-quarters of the distance between 132 and 133. This yields a growth of 32.75%.

4.   A firm plans to pass on an expected productivity increase of 34% over the next 6 years to its employees in higher wages. If it desires to raise wages by the same percentage each time they are adjusted, by what percentage increase per period must it increase wages if the adjustment is made

    (a) once each year?   (d) twice yearly?

    (b) every two years?   (e) every three months?

    (c) every three years?

Answer (a) At the intersection of 6 periods and a final amount of 134 (the level of wage rates after 6 years) Table 1 exhibits a growth rate of 5%. Thus 6 annual increments of 5% will yield a final level of wage rates of 134.

(b) To achieve a final amount of 134 over 3 periods (each of two years) requires a growth at each round at 10.25%. 10.25% is at the inter-section of a final amount of 134 and 3 periods.

(c) If wage rates are adjusted every 3 years there will be two periods. To achieve 134 in two periods requires a growth rate of 15.76% each period.

(d) If wage rates are adjusted half-yearly there will be 12 periods over 6 years. To achieve 134 over 12 periods requires a growth rate in wages of 2.47% each half year.

(e) If wage rates are adjusted quarterly there would be 24 changes in wage rates each of 1.23%.

It will be seen from these examples that if adjustments are made at frequent intervals, then the percentage added is reduced more than proportionately to the shortening of the period. To take the two extremes, cases (c) and (e), the change from an adjustment every three years to one every three months does not reduce the size of each adjustment by a factor of 12, but by one of 12.8.

Table 2. Rates of growth (compounding continuously)

If the growth process is operating continuously (as is usual with economic growth) such that a new amount is compounded at every instant within a period (rather than once each period as in Table 1) then it is appropriate to use this Table of Exponential Growth Rates. Where $\underline{A}$ is the final amount in which an initial quantity of 100 would have grown to in $\underline{t}$ periods, the exponential growth rate $\underline{r}$ per period satisfies the following equation:-

$$A = 100 \times \lim_{n \to \infty} \left(1 + \frac{r}{100.\,n}\right)^{nt}$$

which for real r and integral n yields

$$A = 100 \times e^{rt/100} \text{ (where e is the exponential number, 2.71828...)}$$

demonstrating that for a given final amount the growth rate r for t periods is $1/t$ times the growth rate for 1 period.

This shows the characteristic feature of exponential growth, which is that a given final amount will be reached with a growth-rate of r per cent per period in t periods or by a growth rate of rt in one period, or by any other combination the product of which is rt. One important incidental consequence is that we can express the growth-rate as (for example) 6 per cent per annum or 60 per cent per decade or $\frac{1}{2}$ per cent per month without affecting the final amount, so long as the total time-span over which growth is to take place remains the same.

Although these exponential growth rates are instantaneous, they have to be expressed in finite units of growth and time, the total growth in the unit period being compounded n times at a rate of r/n, where n is a very large number.

As in Table 1 the numbers in the body of the table show the percentage growth per period required to reach the number shown at the left of the row in the number of periods shown at the head of the column.

Examples of use of the Table

1.   If an item grew by 31% in one year, what instantaneous rate of growth (expressed per annum) does this imply?

A growth of 31% corresponds to a final amount of 131 in the left hand column of Table 2. Over one year this gives an instantaneous rate of growth of 27% p.a.

2.   What instantaneous growth rate (expressed per annum) gives rise to an annual growth of 4% ?

A growth of 4% per annum yields a 'final amount' of 104. Scanning down the column appropriate to 1 period in table 2, at the intersection of a 'final amount' of 104 the instantaneous growth rate is 3.92% per annum.

12

3. If the G.N.P. of a country continues to grow at 4% per annum, how long before it doubles?

From question 2 a growth of 4% per annum corresponds to an instantaneous growth rate of growth of 3.92% per annum. To find how many years G.N.P. would double in we scan across the row with a 'final amount' of 200 to seek a growth rate of 3.92%. This appears somewhere between 17 and 18 years. Interpolating backwards we arrive at an answer of 17.7 years.

4. If an item grew by 60% in two years, what instantaneous rate of growth does this imply if expressed at a rate

    (a) per year?

    (b) per half year?

    (c) per quarter?

Answer (a) A growth of 60% in two years corresponds to a 'final amount' of 160 and the number of yearly periods being 2. This yields in Table 2 an instantaneous growth rate of 23.5% per annum.

    (b) If expressed as a rate per half year the number of periods is 4. At the intersection of 4 periods and a final amount of 160 we obtain the instantaneous growth rate of 11.75% per half year.

    (c) If expressed as a rate per quarter the number of periods is 8. To achieve a 'final amount' of 160 in 8 periods (quarters) requires an instantaneous growth rate of 5.88% per quarter.

Note: It will be seen from this example that the instantaneous rate of growth measured per annum is exactly twice the rate of growth measured per half-year, which again is exactly twice the quarterly rate.

Table 1

RATES OF GROWTH

(Compounding each Period)

TABLE 1. RATES OF GROWTH (COMPOUNDING EACH PERIOD)

NUMBER OF PERIODS

FINAL AMOUNT	1	2	3	4	5	6	7	8	9	10
101	1.00	0.50	0.33	0.25	0.20	0.17	0.14	0.12	0.11	0.10
102	2.00	1.00	0.66	0.50	0.40	0.33	0.28	0.25	0.22	0.20
103	3.00	1.49	0.99	0.74	0.59	0.49	0.42	0.37	0.33	0.30
104	4.00	1.98	1.32	0.99	0.79	0.66	0.56	0.49	0.44	0.39
105	5.00	2.47	1.64	1.23	0.98	0.82	0.70	0.61	0.54	0.49
106	6.00	2.96	1.96	1.47	1.17	0.98	0.84	0.73	0.65	0.58
107	7.00	3.44	2.28	1.71	1.36	1.13	0.97	0.85	0.75	0.68
108	8.00	3.92	2.60	1.94	1.55	1.29	1.11	0.97	0.86	0.77
109	9.00	4.40	2.91	2.18	1.74	1.45	1.24	1.08	0.96	0.87
110	10.00	4.88	3.23	2.41	1.92	1.60	1.37	1.20	1.06	0.96
111	11.00	5.36	3.54	2.64	2.11	1.75	1.50	1.31	1.17	1.05
112	12.00	5.83	3.85	2.87	2.29	1.91	1.63	1.43	1.27	1.14
113	13.00	6.30	4.16	3.10	2.47	2.06	1.76	1.54	1.37	1.23
114	14.00	6.77	4.46	3.33	2.66	2.21	1.89	1.65	1.47	1.32
115	15.00	7.24	4.77	3.56	2.83	2.36	2.02	1.76	1.57	1.41
116	16.00	7.70	5.07	3.78	3.01	2.50	2.14	1.87	1.66	1.50
117	17.00	8.17	5.37	4.00	3.19	2.65	2.27	1.98	1.76	1.58
118	18.00	8.63	5.67	4.22	3.37	2.80	2.39	2.09	1.86	1.67
119	19.00	9.09	5.97	4.44	3.54	2.94	2.52	2.20	1.95	1.75
120	20.00	9.54	6.27	4.66	3.71	3.09	2.64	2.31	2.05	1.84
121	21.00	10.00	6.56	4.88	3.89	3.23	2.76	2.41	2.14	1.92
122	22.00	10.45	6.85	5.10	4.06	3.37	2.88	2.52	2.23	2.01
123	23.00	10.91	7.14	5.31	4.23	3.51	3.00	2.62	2.33	2.09
124	24.00	11.36	7.43	5.53	4.40	3.65	3.12	2.73	2.42	2.17
125	25.00	11.80	7.72	5.74	4.56	3.79	3.24	2.83	2.51	2.26
126	26.00	12.25	8.01	5.95	4.73	3.93	3.36	2.93	2.60	2.34
127	27.00	12.69	8.29	6.16	4.90	4.06	3.47	3.03	2.69	2.42
128	28.00	13.14	8.58	6.37	5.06	4.20	3.59	3.13	2.78	2.50
129	29.00	13.58	8.86	6.57	5.22	4.34	3.70	3.23	2.87	2.58
130	30.00	14.02	9.14	6.78	5.39	4.47	3.82	3.33	2.96	2.66
131	31.00	14.46	9.42	6.98	5.55	4.60	3.93	3.43	3.05	2.74
132	32.00	14.89	9.70	7.19	5.71	4.74	4.05	3.53	3.13	2.82
133	33.00	15.33	9.97	7.39	5.87	4.87	4.16	3.63	3.22	2.89
134	34.00	15.76	10.25	7.59	6.03	5.00	4.27	3.73	3.31	2.97
135	35.00	16.19	10.52	7.79	6.19	5.13	4.38	3.82	3.39	3.05
136	36.00	16.62	10.79	7.99	6.34	5.26	4.49	3.92	3.48	3.12
137	37.00	17.05	11.06	8.19	6.50	5.39	4.60	4.01	3.56	3.20
138	38.00	17.47	11.33	8.39	6.65	5.51	4.71	4.11	3.64	3.27
139	39.00	17.90	11.60	8.58	6.81	5.64	4.82	4.20	3.73	3.35
140	40.00	18.32	11.87	8.78	6.96	5.77	4.92	4.30	3.81	3.42
141	41.00	18.74	12.13	8.97	7.11	5.89	5.03	4.39	3.89	3.50
142	42.00	19.16	12.40	9.16	7.26	6.02	5.14	4.48	3.97	3.57
143	43.00	19.58	12.66	9.35	7.42	6.14	5.24	4.57	4.05	3.64
144	44.00	20.00	12.92	9.54	7.57	6.27	5.35	4.66	4.13	3.71
145	45.00	20.42	13.19	9.73	7.71	6.39	5.45	4.75	4.21	3.79
146	46.00	20.83	13.44	9.92	7.86	6.51	5.56	4.84	4.29	3.86
147	47.00	21.24	13.70	10.11	8.01	6.63	5.66	4.93	4.37	3.93
148	48.00	21.66	13.96	10.30	8.16	6.75	5.76	5.02	4.45	4.00
149	49.00	22.07	14.22	10.48	8.30	6.87	5.86	5.11	4.53	4.07
150	50.00	22.47	14.47	10.67	8.45	6.99	5.96	5.20	4.61	4.14

For notes on how to use the table see page 10

TABLE 1.   RATES OF GROWTH   (COMPOUNDING EACH PERIOD)

NUMBER OF PERIODS

FINAL AMOUNT	11	12	13	14	15	16	17	18	19	20
101	0.09	0.08	0.08	0.07	0.07	0.06	0.06	0.06	0.05	0.05
102	0.18	0.17	0.15	0.14	0.13	0.12	0.12	0.11	0.10	0.10
103	0.27	0.25	0.23	0.21	0.20	0.18	0.17	0.16	0.16	0.15
104	0.36	0.33	0.30	0.28	0.26	0.25	0.23	0.22	0.21	0.20
105	0.44	0.41	0.38	0.35	0.33	0.31	0.29	0.27	0.26	0.24
106	0.53	0.49	0.45	0.42	0.39	0.36	0.34	0.32	0.31	0.29
107	0.62	0.57	0.52	0.48	0.45	0.42	0.40	0.38	0.36	0.34
108	0.70	0.64	0.59	0.55	0.51	0.48	0.45	0.43	0.41	0.39
109	0.79	0.72	0.67	0.62	0.58	0.54	0.51	0.48	0.45	0.43
110	0.87	0.80	0.74	0.68	0.64	0.60	0.56	0.53	0.50	0.48
111	0.95	0.87	0.81	0.75	0.70	0.65	0.62	0.58	0.55	0.52
112	1.04	0.95	0.88	0.81	0.76	0.71	0.67	0.63	0.60	0.57
113	1.12	1.02	0.94	0.88	0.82	0.77	0.72	0.68	0.65	0.61
114	1.20	1.10	1.01	0.94	0.88	0.82	0.77	0.73	0.69	0.66
115	1.28	1.17	1.08	1.00	0.94	0.88	0.83	0.78	0.74	0.70
116	1.36	1.24	1.15	1.07	0.99	0.93	0.88	0.83	0.78	0.74
117	1.44	1.32	1.22	1.13	1.05	0.99	0.93	0.88	0.83	0.79
118	1.52	1.39	1.28	1.19	1.11	1.04	0.98	0.92	0.87	0.83
119	1.59	1.46	1.35	1.25	1.17	1.09	1.03	0.97	0.92	0.87
120	1.67	1.53	1.41	1.31	1.22	1.15	1.08	1.02	0.96	0.92
121	1.75	1.60	1.48	1.37	1.28	1.20	1.13	1.06	1.01	0.96
122	1.82	1.67	1.54	1.43	1.33	1.25	1.18	1.11	1.05	1.00
123	1.90	1.74	1.61	1.49	1.39	1.30	1.23	1.16	1.10	1.04
124	1.97	1.81	1.67	1.55	1.44	1.35	1.27	1.20	1.14	1.08
125	2.05	1.88	1.73	1.61	1.50	1.40	1.32	1.25	1.18	1.12
126	2.12	1.94	1.79	1.66	1.55	1.45	1.37	1.29	1.22	1.16
127	2.20	2.01	1.86	1.72	1.61	1.51	1.42	1.34	1.27	1.20
128	2.27	2.08	1.92	1.78	1.66	1.55	1.46	1.38	1.31	1.24
129	2.34	2.14	1.98	1.84	1.71	1.60	1.51	1.42	1.35	1.28
130	2.41	2.21	2.04	1.89	1.76	1.65	1.56	1.47	1.39	1.32
131	2.49	2.28	2.10	1.95	1.82	1.70	1.60	1.51	1.43	1.36
132	2.56	2.34	2.16	2.00	1.87	1.75	1.65	1.55	1.47	1.40
133	2.63	2.40	2.22	2.06	1.92	1.80	1.69	1.60	1.51	1.44
134	2.70	2.47	2.28	2.11	1.97	1.85	1.74	1.64	1.55	1.47
135	2.77	2.53	2.34	2.17	2.02	1.89	1.78	1.68	1.59	1.51
136	2.83	2.60	2.39	2.22	2.07	1.94	1.83	1.72	1.63	1.55
137	2.90	2.66	2.45	2.27	2.12	1.99	1.87	1.76	1.67	1.59
138	2.97	2.72	2.51	2.33	2.17	2.03	1.91	1.81	1.71	1.62
139	3.04	2.78	2.57	2.38	2.22	2.08	1.96	1.85	1.75	1.66
140	3.11	2.84	2.62	2.43	2.27	2.13	2.00	1.89	1.79	1.70
141	3.17	2.90	2.68	2.48	2.32	2.17	2.04	1.93	1.82	1.73
142	3.24	2.97	2.73	2.54	2.37	2.22	2.08	1.97	1.86	1.77
143	3.31	3.03	2.79	2.59	2.41	2.26	2.13	2.01	1.90	1.80
144	3.37	3.09	2.84	2.64	2.46	2.31	2.17	2.05	1.94	1.84
145	3.44	3.14	2.90	2.69	2.51	2.35	2.21	2.09	1.97	1.88
146	3.50	3.20	2.95	2.74	2.56	2.39	2.25	2.12	2.01	1.91
147	3.56	3.26	3.01	2.79	2.60	2.44	2.29	2.16	2.05	1.94
148	3.63	3.32	3.06	2.84	2.65	2.48	2.33	2.20	2.08	1.98
149	3.69	3.38	3.12	2.89	2.69	2.52	2.37	2.24	2.12	2.01
150	3.75	3.44	3.17	2.94	2.74	2.57	2.41	2.28	2.16	2.05

For notes on how to use the table see page 10

TABLE 1. RATES OF GROWTH (COMPOUNDING EACH PERIOD)

NUMBER OF PERIODS

FINAL AMOUNT	21	22	23	24	25	26	27	28	29	30
101	0.05	0.05	0.04	0.04	0.04	0.04	0.04	0.04	0.03	0.03
102	0.09	0.09	0.09	0.08	0.08	0.08	0.07	0.07	0.07	0.07
103	0.14	0.13	0.13	0.12	0.12	0.11	0.11	0.11	0.10	0.10
104	0.19	0.18	0.17	0.16	0.16	0.15	0.15	0.14	0.14	0.13
105	0.23	0.22	0.21	0.20	0.20	0.19	0.18	0.17	0.17	0.16
106	0.28	0.27	0.25	0.24	0.23	0.22	0.22	0.21	0.20	0.19
107	0.32	0.31	0.29	0.28	0.27	0.26	0.25	0.24	0.23	0.23
108	0.37	0.35	0.34	0.32	0.31	0.30	0.29	0.28	0.27	0.26
109	0.41	0.39	0.38	0.36	0.35	0.33	0.32	0.31	0.30	0.29
110	0.45	0.43	0.42	0.40	0.38	0.37	0.35	0.34	0.33	0.32
111	0.50	0.48	0.45	0.44	0.42	0.40	0.39	0.37	0.36	0.35
112	0.54	0.52	0.49	0.47	0.45	0.44	0.42	0.41	0.39	0.38
113	0.58	0.56	0.53	0.51	0.49	0.47	0.45	0.44	0.42	0.41
114	0.63	0.60	0.57	0.55	0.53	0.51	0.49	0.47	0.45	0.44
115	0.67	0.64	0.61	0.58	0.56	0.54	0.52	0.50	0.48	0.47
116	0.71	0.68	0.65	0.62	0.60	0.57	0.55	0.53	0.51	0.50
117	0.75	0.72	0.68	0.66	0.63	0.61	0.58	0.56	0.54	0.52
118	0.79	0.76	0.72	0.69	0.66	0.64	0.61	0.59	0.57	0.55
119	0.83	0.79	0.76	0.73	0.70	0.67	0.65	0.62	0.60	0.58
120	0.87	0.83	0.80	0.76	0.73	0.70	0.68	0.65	0.63	0.61
121	0.91	0.87	0.83	0.80	0.77	0.74	0.71	0.68	0.66	0.64
122	0.95	0.91	0.87	0.83	0.80	0.77	0.74	0.71	0.69	0.67
123	0.99	0.95	0.90	0.87	0.83	0.80	0.77	0.74	0.72	0.69
124	1.03	0.98	0.94	0.90	0.86	0.83	0.80	0.77	0.74	0.72
125	1.07	1.02	0.97	0.93	0.90	0.86	0.83	0.80	0.77	0.75
126	1.11	1.06	1.01	0.97	0.93	0.89	0.86	0.83	0.80	0.77
127	1.14	1.09	1.04	1.00	0.96	0.92	0.89	0.86	0.83	0.80
128	1.18	1.13	1.08	1.03	0.99	0.95	0.92	0.89	0.85	0.83
129	1.22	1.16	1.11	1.07	1.02	0.98	0.95	0.91	0.88	0.85
130	1.26	1.20	1.15	1.10	1.05	1.01	0.98	0.94	0.91	0.88
131	1.29	1.23	1.18	1.13	1.09	1.04	1.01	0.97	0.94	0.90
132	1.33	1.27	1.21	1.16	1.12	1.07	1.03	1.00	0.96	0.93
133	1.37	1.30	1.25	1.20	1.15	1.10	1.06	1.02	0.99	0.96
134	1.40	1.34	1.28	1.23	1.18	1.13	1.09	1.05	1.01	0.98
135	1.44	1.37	1.31	1.26	1.21	1.16	1.12	1.08	1.04	1.01
136	1.47	1.41	1.35	1.29	1.24	1.19	1.15	1.10	1.07	1.03
137	1.51	1.44	1.38	1.32	1.27	1.22	1.17	1.13	1.09	1.05
138	1.55	1.47	1.41	1.35	1.30	1.25	1.20	1.16	1.12	1.08
139	1.58	1.51	1.44	1.38	1.33	1.27	1.23	1.18	1.14	1.10
140	1.62	1.54	1.47	1.41	1.35	1.30	1.25	1.21	1.17	1.13
141	1.65	1.57	1.51	1.44	1.38	1.33	1.28	1.23	1.19	1.15
142	1.68	1.61	1.54	1.47	1.41	1.36	1.31	1.26	1.22	1.18
143	1.72	1.64	1.57	1.50	1.44	1.39	1.33	1.29	1.24	1.20
144	1.75	1.67	1.60	1.53	1.47	1.41	1.36	1.31	1.27	1.22
145	1.79	1.70	1.63	1.56	1.50	1.44	1.39	1.34	1.29	1.25
146	1.82	1.74	1.66	1.59	1.53	1.47	1.41	1.36	1.31	1.27
147	1.85	1.77	1.69	1.62	1.55	1.49	1.44	1.39	1.34	1.29
148	1.88	1.80	1.72	1.65	1.58	1.52	1.46	1.41	1.36	1.32
149	1.92	1.83	1.75	1.68	1.61	1.55	1.49	1.43	1.38	1.34
150	1.95	1.86	1.78	1.70	1.64	1.57	1.51	1.46	1.41	1.36

For notes on how to use the table see page 10

TABLE 1. RATES OF GROWTH (COMPOUNDING EACH PERIOD)

NUMBER OF PERIODS

FINAL AMOUNT	31	32	33	34	35	36	37	38	39	40
101	0.03	0.03	0.03	0.03	0.03	0.03	0.03	0.03	0.03	0.02
102	0.06	0.06	0.06	0.06	0.06	0.06	0.05	0.05	0.05	0.05
103	0.10	0.09	0.09	0.09	0.08	0.08	0.08	0.08	0.08	0.07
104	0.13	0.12	0.12	0.12	0.11	0.11	0.11	0.10	0.10	0.10
105	0.16	0.15	0.15	0.14	0.14	0.14	0.13	0.13	0.13	0.12
106	0.19	0.18	0.18	0.17	0.17	0.16	0.16	0.15	0.15	0.15
107	0.22	0.21	0.21	0.20	0.19	0.19	0.18	0.18	0.17	0.17
108	0.25	0.24	0.23	0.23	0.22	0.21	0.21	0.20	0.20	0.19
109	0.28	0.27	0.26	0.25	0.25	0.24	0.23	0.23	0.22	0.22
110	0.31	0.30	0.29	0.28	0.27	0.27	0.26	0.25	0.24	0.24
111	0.34	0.33	0.32	0.31	0.30	0.29	0.28	0.28	0.27	0.26
112	0.37	0.35	0.34	0.33	0.32	0.32	0.31	0.30	0.29	0.28
113	0.40	0.38	0.37	0.36	0.35	0.34	0.33	0.32	0.31	0.31
114	0.42	0.41	0.40	0.39	0.38	0.36	0.35	0.35	0.34	0.33
115	0.45	0.44	0.42	0.41	0.40	0.39	0.38	0.37	0.36	0.35
116	0.48	0.46	0.45	0.44	0.42	0.41	0.40	0.39	0.38	0.37
117	0.51	0.49	0.48	0.46	0.45	0.44	0.43	0.41	0.40	0.39
118	0.54	0.52	0.50	0.49	0.47	0.46	0.45	0.44	0.43	0.41
119	0.56	0.55	0.53	0.51	0.50	0.48	0.47	0.46	0.45	0.44
120	0.59	0.57	0.55	0.54	0.52	0.51	0.49	0.48	0.47	0.46
121	0.62	0.60	0.58	0.56	0.55	0.53	0.52	0.50	0.49	0.48
122	0.64	0.62	0.60	0.59	0.57	0.55	0.54	0.52	0.51	0.50
123	0.67	0.65	0.63	0.61	0.59	0.58	0.56	0.55	0.53	0.52
124	0.70	0.67	0.65	0.63	0.62	0.60	0.58	0.57	0.55	0.54
125	0.72	0.70	0.68	0.66	0.64	0.62	0.60	0.59	0.57	0.56
126	0.75	0.72	0.70	0.68	0.66	0.64	0.63	0.61	0.59	0.58
127	0.77	0.75	0.73	0.71	0.69	0.67	0.65	0.63	0.61	0.60
128	0.80	0.77	0.75	0.73	0.71	0.69	0.67	0.65	0.63	0.62
129	0.82	0.80	0.77	0.75	0.73	0.71	0.69	0.67	0.66	0.64
130	0.85	0.82	0.80	0.77	0.75	0.73	0.71	0.69	0.67	0.66
131	0.87	0.85	0.82	0.80	0.77	0.75	0.73	0.71	0.69	0.68
132	0.90	0.87	0.84	0.82	0.80	0.77	0.75	0.73	0.71	0.70
133	0.92	0.90	0.87	0.84	0.82	0.80	0.77	0.75	0.73	0.72
134	0.95	0.92	0.89	0.86	0.84	0.82	0.79	0.77	0.75	0.73
135	0.97	0.94	0.91	0.89	0.86	0.84	0.81	0.79	0.77	0.75
136	1.00	0.97	0.94	0.91	0.88	0.86	0.83	0.81	0.79	0.77
137	1.02	0.99	0.96	0.93	0.90	0.88	0.85	0.83	0.81	0.79
138	1.04	1.01	0.98	0.95	0.92	0.90	0.87	0.85	0.83	0.81
139	1.07	1.03	1.00	0.97	0.95	0.92	0.89	0.87	0.85	0.83
140	1.09	1.06	1.02	0.99	0.97	0.94	0.91	0.89	0.87	0.84
141	1.11	1.08	1.05	1.02	0.99	0.96	0.93	0.91	0.88	0.86
142	1.14	1.10	1.07	1.04	1.01	0.98	0.95	0.93	0.90	0.88
143	1.16	1.12	1.09	1.06	1.03	1.00	0.97	0.95	0.92	0.90
144	1.18	1.15	1.11	1.08	1.05	1.02	0.99	0.96	0.94	0.92
145	1.21	1.17	1.13	1.10	1.07	1.04	1.01	0.98	0.96	0.93
146	1.23	1.19	1.15	1.12	1.09	1.06	1.03	1.00	0.98	0.95
147	1.25	1.21	1.17	1.14	1.11	1.08	1.05	1.02	0.99	0.97
148	1.27	1.23	1.20	1.16	1.13	1.09	1.07	1.04	1.01	0.98
149	1.29	1.25	1.22	1.18	1.15	1.11	1.08	1.05	1.03	1.00
150	1.32	1.28	1.24	1.20	1.17	1.13	1.10	1.07	1.05	1.02

For notes on how to use the table see page 10

TABLE 1. RATES OF GROWTH (COMPOUNDING EACH PERIOD)

NUMBER OF PERIODS

FINAL AMOUNT	41	42	43	44	45	46	47	48	49	50
101	0.02	0.02	0.02	0.02	0.02	0.02	0.02	0.02	0.02	0.02
102	0.05	0.05	0.05	0.05	0.04	0.04	0.04	0.04	0.04	0.04
103	0.07	0.07	0.07	0.07	0.07	0.06	0.06	0.06	0.06	0.06
104	0.10	0.09	0.09	0.09	0.09	0.09	0.08	0.08	0.08	0.08
105	0.12	0.12	0.11	0.11	0.11	0.11	0.10	0.10	0.10	0.10
106	0.14	0.14	0.14	0.13	0.13	0.13	0.12	0.12	0.12	0.12
107	0.17	0.16	0.16	0.15	0.15	0.15	0.14	0.14	0.14	0.14
108	0.19	0.18	0.18	0.18	0.17	0.17	0.16	0.16	0.16	0.15
109	0.21	0.21	0.20	0.20	0.19	0.19	0.18	0.18	0.18	0.17
110	0.23	0.23	0.22	0.22	0.21	0.21	0.20	0.20	0.19	0.19
111	0.25	0.25	0.24	0.24	0.23	0.23	0.22	0.22	0.21	0.21
112	0.28	0.27	0.26	0.26	0.25	0.25	0.24	0.24	0.23	0.23
113	0.30	0.29	0.28	0.28	0.27	0.27	0.26	0.25	0.25	0.24
114	0.32	0.31	0.31	0.30	0.29	0.29	0.28	0.27	0.27	0.26
115	0.34	0.33	0.33	0.32	0.31	0.30	0.30	0.29	0.29	0.28
116	0.36	0.35	0.35	0.34	0.33	0.32	0.32	0.31	0.30	0.30
117	0.38	0.37	0.37	0.36	0.35	0.34	0.33	0.33	0.32	0.31
118	0.40	0.39	0.39	0.38	0.37	0.36	0.35	0.35	0.34	0.33
119	0.43	0.42	0.41	0.40	0.39	0.38	0.37	0.36	0.36	0.35
120	0.45	0.44	0.42	0.42	0.41	0.40	0.39	0.38	0.37	0.37
121	0.47	0.45	0.44	0.43	0.42	0.42	0.41	0.40	0.39	0.38
122	0.49	0.47	0.46	0.45	0.44	0.43	0.42	0.42	0.41	0.40
123	0.51	0.49	0.48	0.47	0.46	0.45	0.44	0.43	0.42	0.41
124	0.53	0.51	0.50	0.49	0.48	0.47	0.46	0.45	0.44	0.43
125	0.55	0.53	0.52	0.51	0.50	0.49	0.48	0.47	0.46	0.45
126	0.57	0.55	0.54	0.53	0.51	0.50	0.49	0.48	0.47	0.46
127	0.58	0.57	0.56	0.54	0.53	0.52	0.51	0.50	0.49	0.48
128	0.60	0.59	0.58	0.56	0.55	0.54	0.53	0.52	0.51	0.49
129	0.62	0.61	0.59	0.58	0.57	0.56	0.54	0.53	0.52	0.51
130	0.64	0.63	0.61	0.60	0.58	0.57	0.56	0.55	0.54	0.53
131	0.66	0.64	0.63	0.62	0.60	0.59	0.58	0.56	0.55	0.54
132	0.68	0.66	0.65	0.63	0.62	0.61	0.59	0.58	0.57	0.56
133	0.70	0.68	0.67	0.65	0.64	0.62	0.61	0.60	0.58	0.57
134	0.72	0.70	0.68	0.67	0.65	0.64	0.62	0.61	0.60	0.59
135	0.73	0.72	0.70	0.68	0.67	0.65	0.64	0.63	0.61	0.60
136	0.75	0.73	0.72	0.70	0.69	0.67	0.66	0.64	0.63	0.62
137	0.77	0.75	0.73	0.72	0.70	0.69	0.67	0.66	0.64	0.63
138	0.79	0.77	0.75	0.73	0.72	0.70	0.69	0.67	0.66	0.65
139	0.81	0.79	0.77	0.75	0.73	0.72	0.70	0.69	0.67	0.66
140	0.82	0.80	0.79	0.77	0.75	0.73	0.72	0.70	0.69	0.68
141	0.84	0.82	0.80	0.78	0.77	0.75	0.73	0.72	0.70	0.69
142	0.86	0.84	0.82	0.80	0.78	0.77	0.75	0.73	0.72	0.70
143	0.88	0.86	0.84	0.82	0.80	0.78	0.76	0.75	0.73	0.72
144	0.89	0.87	0.85	0.83	0.81	0.80	0.78	0.76	0.75	0.73
145	0.91	0.89	0.87	0.85	0.83	0.81	0.79	0.78	0.76	0.75
146	0.93	0.91	0.88	0.86	0.84	0.83	0.81	0.79	0.78	0.76
147	0.94	0.92	0.90	0.88	0.86	0.84	0.82	0.81	0.79	0.77
148	0.96	0.94	0.92	0.89	0.88	0.86	0.84	0.82	0.80	0.79
149	0.98	0.95	0.93	0.91	0.89	0.87	0.85	0.83	0.82	0.80
150	0.99	0.97	0.95	0.93	0.91	0.89	0.87	0.85	0.83	0.81

For notes on how to use the table see page 10

TABLE 1. RATES OF GROWTH (COMPOUNDING EACH PERIOD)

NUMBER OF PERIODS

FINAL AMOUNT	60	70	80	90	100	120	140	160	180	200
101	0.02	0.01	0.01	0.01	0.01	0.01	0.01	0.01	0.01	0.00
102	0.03	0.03	0.02	0.02	0.02	0.02	0.01	0.01	0.01	0.01
103	0.05	0.04	0.04	0.03	0.03	0.02	0.02	0.02	0.02	0.01
104	0.07	0.06	0.05	0.04	0.04	0.03	0.03	0.02	0.02	0.02
105	0.08	0.07	0.06	0.05	0.05	0.04	0.03	0.03	0.03	0.02
106	0.10	0.08	0.07	0.06	0.06	0.05	0.04	0.04	0.03	0.03
107	0.11	0.10	0.08	0.08	0.07	0.06	0.05	0.04	0.04	0.03
108	0.13	0.11	0.10	0.09	0.08	0.06	0.05	0.05	0.04	0.04
109	0.14	0.12	0.11	0.10	0.09	0.07	0.06	0.05	0.05	0.04
110	0.16	0.14	0.12	0.11	0.10	0.08	0.07	0.06	0.05	0.05
111	0.17	0.15	0.13	0.12	0.10	0.09	0.07	0.07	0.06	0.05
112	0.19	0.16	0.14	0.13	0.11	0.09	0.08	0.07	0.06	0.06
113	0.20	0.17	0.15	0.14	0.12	0.10	0.09	0.08	0.07	0.06
114	0.22	0.19	0.16	0.15	0.13	0.11	0.09	0.08	0.07	0.07
115	0.23	0.20	0.17	0.16	0.14	0.12	0.10	0.09	0.08	0.07
116	0.25	0.21	0.19	0.17	0.15	0.12	0.11	0.09	0.08	0.07
117	0.26	0.22	0.20	0.17	0.16	0.13	0.11	0.10	0.09	0.08
118	0.28	0.24	0.21	0.18	0.17	0.14	0.12	0.10	0.09	0.08
119	0.29	0.25	0.22	0.19	0.17	0.15	0.12	0.11	0.10	0.09
120	0.30	0.26	0.23	0.20	0.18	0.15	0.13	0.11	0.10	0.09
121	0.32	0.27	0.24	0.21	0.19	0.16	0.14	0.12	0.11	0.10
122	0.33	0.28	0.25	0.22	0.20	0.17	0.14	0.12	0.11	0.10
123	0.35	0.30	0.26	0.23	0.21	0.17	0.15	0.13	0.12	0.10
124	0.36	0.31	0.27	0.24	0.22	0.18	0.15	0.13	0.12	0.11
125	0.37	0.32	0.28	0.25	0.22	0.19	0.16	0.14	0.12	0.11
126	0.39	0.33	0.29	0.26	0.23	0.19	0.17	0.14	0.13	0.12
127	0.40	0.34	0.30	0.27	0.24	0.20	0.17	0.15	0.13	0.12
128	0.41	0.35	0.31	0.27	0.25	0.21	0.18	0.15	0.14	0.12
129	0.43	0.36	0.32	0.28	0.25	0.21	0.18	0.16	0.14	0.13
130	0.44	0.38	0.33	0.29	0.26	0.22	0.19	0.16	0.15	0.13
131	0.45	0.39	0.34	0.30	0.27	0.23	0.19	0.17	0.15	0.14
132	0.46	0.40	0.35	0.31	0.28	0.23	0.20	0.17	0.15	0.14
133	0.48	0.41	0.36	0.32	0.29	0.24	0.20	0.18	0.16	0.14
134	0.49	0.42	0.37	0.33	0.29	0.24	0.21	0.18	0.16	0.15
135	0.50	0.43	0.38	0.33	0.30	0.25	0.21	0.19	0.17	0.15
136	0.51	0.44	0.39	0.34	0.31	0.26	0.22	0.19	0.17	0.15
137	0.53	0.45	0.39	0.35	0.32	0.26	0.23	0.20	0.18	0.16
138	0.54	0.46	0.40	0.36	0.32	0.27	0.23	0.20	0.18	0.16
139	0.55	0.47	0.41	0.37	0.33	0.27	0.24	0.21	0.18	0.16
140	0.56	0.48	0.42	0.37	0.34	0.28	0.24	0.21	0.19	0.17
141	0.57	0.49	0.43	0.38	0.34	0.29	0.25	0.21	0.19	0.17
142	0.59	0.50	0.44	0.39	0.35	0.29	0.25	0.22	0.19	0.18
143	0.60	0.51	0.45	0.40	0.36	0.30	0.26	0.22	0.20	0.18
144	0.61	0.52	0.46	0.41	0.37	0.30	0.26	0.23	0.20	0.18
145	0.62	0.53	0.47	0.41	0.37	0.31	0.27	0.23	0.21	0.19
146	0.63	0.54	0.47	0.42	0.38	0.32	0.27	0.24	0.21	0.19
147	0.64	0.55	0.48	0.43	0.39	0.32	0.28	0.24	0.21	0.19
148	0.66	0.56	0.49	0.44	0.39	0.33	0.28	0.25	0.22	0.20
149	0.67	0.57	0.50	0.44	0.40	0.33	0.29	0.25	0.22	0.20
150	0.68	0.58	0.51	0.45	0.41	0.34	0.29	0.25	0.23	0.20

For notes on how to use the table see page 10

TABLE 1. RATES OF GROWTH (COMPOUNDING EACH PERIOD)

NUMBER OF PERIODS

FINAL AMOUNT	1	2	3	4	5	6	7	8	9	10
151	51.00	22.88	14.73	10.85	8.59	7.11	6.06	5.29	4.69	4.21
152	52.00	23.29	14.98	11.04	8.73	7.23	6.16	5.37	4.76	4.28
153	53.00	23.69	15.23	11.22	8.88	7.35	6.26	5.46	4.84	4.34
154	54.00	24.10	15.48	11.40	9.02	7.46	6.36	5.55	4.91	4.41
155	55.00	24.50	15.73	11.58	9.16	7.58	6.46	5.63	4.99	4.48
156	56.00	24.90	15.98	11.76	9.30	7.69	6.56	5.72	5.07	4.55
157	57.00	25.30	16.23	11.94	9.44	7.81	6.66	5.80	5.14	4.61
158	58.00	25.70	16.47	12.12	9.58	7.92	6.75	5.88	5.21	4.68
159	59.00	26.10	16.72	12.29	9.72	8.04	6.85	5.97	5.29	4.75
160	60.00	26.49	16.96	12.47	9.86	8.15	6.94	6.05	5.36	4.81
161	61.00	26.89	17.20	12.64	9.99	8.26	7.04	6.13	5.43	4.88
162	62.00	27.28	17.45	12.82	10.13	8.37	7.13	6.22	5.51	4.94
163	63.00	27.67	17.69	12.99	10.26	8.48	7.23	6.30	5.58	5.01
164	64.00	28.06	17.93	13.16	10.40	8.59	7.32	6.38	5.65	5.07
165	65.00	28.45	18.17	13.34	10.53	8.70	7.42	6.46	5.72	5.14
166	66.00	28.84	18.40	13.51	10.67	8.81	7.51	6.54	5.79	5.20
167	67.00	29.23	18.64	13.68	10.80	8.92	7.60	6.62	5.86	5.26
168	68.00	29.61	18.88	13.85	10.93	9.03	7.69	6.70	5.93	5.32
169	69.00	30.00	19.11	14.02	11.07	9.14	7.78	6.78	6.00	5.39
170	70.00	30.38	19.35	14.19	11.20	9.25	7.88	6.86	6.07	5.45
171	71.00	30.77	19.58	14.35	11.33	9.35	7.97	6.94	6.14	5.51
172	72.00	31.15	19.81	14.52	11.46	9.46	8.06	7.01	6.21	5.57
173	73.00	31.53	20.05	14.69	11.59	9.57	8.15	7.09	6.28	5.63
174	74.00	31.91	20.28	14.85	11.71	9.67	8.23	7.17	6.35	5.70
175	75.00	32.29	20.51	15.02	11.84	9.78	8.32	7.25	6.42	5.76
176	76.00	32.66	20.74	15.18	11.97	9.88	8.41	7.32	6.48	5.82
177	77.00	33.04	20.96	15.34	12.10	9.98	8.50	7.40	6.55	5.88
178	78.00	33.42	21.19	15.51	12.22	10.09	8.59	7.47	6.62	5.94
179	79.00	33.79	21.42	15.67	12.35	10.19	8.67	7.55	6.68	5.99
180	80.00	34.16	21.64	15.83	12.47	10.29	8.76	7.62	6.75	6.05
181	81.00	34.54	21.87	15.99	12.60	10.39	8.85	7.70	6.81	6.11
182	82.00	34.91	22.09	16.15	12.72	10.50	8.93	7.77	6.88	6.17
183	83.00	35.28	22.32	16.31	12.85	10.60	9.02	7.85	6.95	6.23
184	84.00	35.65	22.54	16.47	12.97	10.70	9.10	7.92	7.01	6.29
185	85.00	36.01	22.76	16.63	13.09	10.80	9.19	7.99	7.07	6.35
186	86.00	36.38	22.98	16.78	13.21	10.90	9.27	8.07	7.14	6.40
187	87.00	36.75	23.20	16.94	13.34	11.00	9.35	8.14	7.20	6.46
188	88.00	37.11	23.42	17.10	13.46	11.09	9.44	8.21	7.27	6.52
189	89.00	37.48	23.64	17.25	13.58	11.19	9.52	8.28	7.33	6.57
190	90.00	37.84	23.86	17.41	13.70	11.29	9.60	8.35	7.39	6.63
191	91.00	38.20	24.07	17.56	13.82	11.39	9.69	8.42	7.45	6.68
192	92.00	38.56	24.29	17.71	13.94	11.49	9.77	8.50	7.52	6.74
193	93.00	38.92	24.50	17.87	14.05	11.58	9.85	8.57	7.58	6.80
194	94.00	39.28	24.72	18.02	14.17	11.68	9.93	8.64	7.64	6.85
195	95.00	39.64	24.93	18.17	14.29	11.77	10.01	8.71	7.70	6.91
196	96.00	40.00	25.15	18.32	14.41	11.87	10.09	8.78	7.76	6.96
197	97.00	40.36	25.36	18.47	14.52	11.96	10.17	8.84	7.82	7.02
198	98.00	40.71	25.57	18.62	14.64	12.06	10.25	8.91	7.89	7.07
199	99.00	41.07	25.78	18.77	14.75	12.15	10.33	8.98	7.95	7.12
200		41.42	25.99	18.92	14.87	12.25	10.41	9.05	8.01	7.18

For notes on how to use the table see page 10

TABLE 1. RATES OF GROWTH (COMPOUNDING EACH PERIOD)

NUMBER OF PERIODS

FINAL AMOUNT	11	12	13	14	15	16	17	18	19	20
151	3.82	3.49	3.22	2.99	2.79	2.61	2.45	2.32	2.19	2.08
152	3.88	3.55	3.27	3.04	2.83	2.65	2.49	2.35	2.23	2.12
153	3.94	3.61	3.33	3.08	2.88	2.69	2.53	2.39	2.26	2.15
154	4.00	3.66	3.38	3.13	2.92	2.74	2.57	2.43	2.30	2.18
155	4.06	3.72	3.43	3.18	2.96	2.78	2.61	2.46	2.33	2.22
156	4.13	3.78	3.48	3.23	3.01	2.82	2.65	2.50	2.37	2.25
157	4.19	3.83	3.53	3.27	3.05	2.86	2.69	2.54	2.40	2.28
158	4.25	3.89	3.58	3.32	3.10	2.90	2.73	2.57	2.44	2.31
159	4.31	3.94	3.63	3.37	3.14	2.94	2.77	2.61	2.47	2.35
160	4.37	3.99	3.68	3.41	3.18	2.98	2.80	2.65	2.50	2.38
161	4.42	4.05	3.73	3.46	3.23	3.02	2.84	2.68	2.54	2.41
162	4.48	4.10	3.78	3.51	3.27	3.06	2.88	2.72	2.57	2.44
163	4.54	4.16	3.83	3.55	3.31	3.10	2.92	2.75	2.60	2.47
164	4.60	4.21	3.88	3.60	3.35	3.14	2.95	2.79	2.64	2.50
165	4.66	4.26	3.93	3.64	3.39	3.18	2.99	2.82	2.67	2.54
166	4.72	4.31	3.98	3.69	3.44	3.22	3.03	2.86	2.70	2.57
167	4.77	4.37	4.02	3.73	3.48	3.26	3.06	2.89	2.74	2.60
168	4.83	4.42	4.07	3.78	3.52	3.30	3.10	2.92	2.77	2.63
169	4.89	4.47	4.12	3.82	3.56	3.33	3.13	2.96	2.80	2.66
170	4.94	4.52	4.17	3.86	3.60	3.37	3.17	2.99	2.83	2.69
171	5.00	4.57	4.21	3.91	3.64	3.41	3.21	3.03	2.86	2.72
172	5.05	4.62	4.26	3.95	3.68	3.45	3.24	3.06	2.90	2.75
173	5.11	4.67	4.31	3.99	3.72	3.49	3.28	3.09	2.93	2.78
174	5.16	4.72	4.35	4.04	3.76	3.52	3.31	3.12	2.96	2.81
175	5.22	4.77	4.40	4.08	3.80	3.56	3.35	3.16	2.99	2.84
176	5.27	4.82	4.44	4.12	3.84	3.60	3.38	3.19	3.02	2.87
177	5.33	4.87	4.49	4.16	3.88	3.63	3.42	3.22	3.05	2.90
178	5.38	4.92	4.54	4.20	3.92	3.67	3.45	3.26	3.08	2.93
179	5.44	4.97	4.58	4.25	3.96	3.71	3.48	3.29	3.11	2.95
180	5.49	5.02	4.63	4.29	4.00	3.74	3.52	3.32	3.14	2.98
181	5.54	5.07	4.67	4.33	4.03	3.78	3.55	3.35	3.17	3.01
182	5.59	5.12	4.71	4.37	4.07	3.81	3.59	3.38	3.20	3.04
183	5.65	5.16	4.76	4.41	4.11	3.85	3.62	3.41	3.23	3.07
184	5.70	5.21	4.80	4.45	4.15	3.88	3.65	3.45	3.26	3.10
185	5.75	5.26	4.85	4.49	4.19	3.92	3.69	3.48	3.29	3.12
186	5.80	5.31	4.89	4.53	4.22	3.95	3.72	3.51	3.32	3.15
187	5.86	5.35	4.93	4.57	4.26	3.99	3.75	3.54	3.35	3.18
188	5.91	5.40	4.98	4.61	4.30	4.02	3.78	3.57	3.38	3.21
189	5.96	5.45	5.02	4.65	4.34	4.06	3.82	3.60	3.41	3.23
190	6.01	5.49	5.06	4.69	4.37	4.09	3.85	3.63	3.44	3.26
191	6.06	5.54	5.10	4.73	4.41	4.13	3.88	3.66	3.46	3.29
192	6.11	5.59	5.15	4.77	4.44	4.16	3.91	3.69	3.49	3.32
193	6.16	5.63	5.19	4.81	4.48	4.20	3.94	3.72	3.52	3.34
194	6.21	5.68	5.23	4.85	4.52	4.23	3.98	3.75	3.55	3.37
195	6.26	5.72	5.27	4.89	4.55	4.26	4.01	3.78	3.58	3.40
196	6.31	5.77	5.31	4.92	4.59	4.30	4.04	3.81	3.61	3.42
197	6.36	5.81	5.35	4.96	4.62	4.33	4.07	3.84	3.63	3.45
198	6.41	5.86	5.40	5.00	4.66	4.36	4.10	3.87	3.66	3.47
199	6.46	5.90	5.44	5.04	4.69	4.39	4.13	3.90	3.69	3.50
200	6.50	5.95	5.48	5.08	4.73	4.43	4.16	3.93	3.72	3.53

For notes on how to use the table see page 10

24

TABLE 1. RATES OF GROWTH (COMPOUNDING EACH PERIOD)

NUMBER OF PERIODS

FINAL AMOUNT	21	22	23	24	25	26	27	28	29	30
151	1.98	1.89	1.81	1.73	1.66	1.60	1.54	1.48	1.43	1.38
152	2.01	1.92	1.84	1.76	1.69	1.62	1.56	1.51	1.45	1.41
153	2.05	1.95	1.87	1.79	1.72	1.65	1.59	1.53	1.48	1.43
154	2.08	1.98	1.90	1.82	1.74	1.67	1.61	1.55	1.50	1.45
155	2.11	2.01	1.92	1.84	1.77	1.70	1.64	1.58	1.52	1.47
156	2.14	2.04	1.95	1.87	1.79	1.73	1.66	1.60	1.55	1.49
157	2.17	2.07	1.98	1.90	1.82	1.75	1.68	1.62	1.57	1.51
158	2.20	2.10	2.01	1.92	1.85	1.77	1.71	1.65	1.59	1.54
159	2.23	2.13	2.04	1.95	1.87	1.80	1.73	1.67	1.61	1.56
160	2.26	2.16	2.06	1.98	1.90	1.82	1.76	1.69	1.63	1.58
161	2.29	2.19	2.09	2.00	1.92	1.85	1.78	1.72	1.66	1.60
162	2.32	2.22	2.12	2.03	1.95	1.87	1.80	1.74	1.68	1.62
163	2.35	2.25	2.15	2.06	1.97	1.90	1.83	1.76	1.70	1.64
164	2.38	2.27	2.17	2.08	2.00	1.92	1.85	1.78	1.72	1.66
165	2.41	2.30	2.20	2.11	2.02	1.94	1.87	1.80	1.74	1.68
166	2.44	2.33	2.23	2.13	2.05	1.97	1.89	1.83	1.76	1.70
167	2.47	2.36	2.25	2.16	2.07	1.99	1.92	1.85	1.78	1.72
168	2.50	2.39	2.28	2.19	2.10	2.02	1.94	1.87	1.81	1.74
169	2.53	2.41	2.31	2.21	2.12	2.04	1.96	1.89	1.83	1.76
170	2.56	2.44	2.33	2.24	2.15	2.06	1.98	1.91	1.85	1.78
171	2.59	2.47	2.36	2.26	2.17	2.08	2.01	1.93	1.87	1.80
172	2.62	2.50	2.39	2.29	2.19	2.11	2.03	1.96	1.89	1.82
173	2.64	2.52	2.41	2.31	2.22	2.13	2.05	1.98	1.91	1.84
174	2.67	2.55	2.44	2.33	2.24	2.15	2.07	2.00	1.93	1.86
175	2.70	2.58	2.46	2.36	2.26	2.18	2.09	2.02	1.95	1.88
176	2.73	2.60	2.49	2.38	2.29	2.20	2.12	2.04	1.97	1.90
177	2.76	2.63	2.51	2.41	2.31	2.22	2.14	2.06	1.99	1.92
178	2.78	2.66	2.54	2.43	2.33	2.24	2.16	2.08	2.01	1.94
179	2.81	2.68	2.56	2.46	2.36	2.26	2.18	2.10	2.03	1.96
180	2.84	2.71	2.59	2.48	2.38	2.29	2.20	2.12	2.05	1.98
181	2.87	2.73	2.61	2.50	2.40	2.31	2.22	2.14	2.07	2.00
182	2.89	2.76	2.64	2.53	2.42	2.33	2.24	2.16	2.09	2.02
183	2.92	2.78	2.66	2.55	2.45	2.35	2.26	2.18	2.11	2.03
184	2.95	2.81	2.69	2.57	2.47	2.37	2.28	2.20	2.12	2.05
185	2.97	2.84	2.71	2.60	2.49	2.39	2.30	2.22	2.14	2.07
186	3.00	2.86	2.73	2.62	2.51	2.42	2.33	2.24	2.16	2.09
187	3.03	2.89	2.76	2.64	2.54	2.44	2.35	2.26	2.18	2.11
188	3.05	2.91	2.78	2.67	2.56	2.46	2.37	2.28	2.20	2.13
189	3.08	2.94	2.81	2.69	2.58	2.48	2.39	2.30	2.22	2.14
190	3.10	2.96	2.83	2.71	2.60	2.50	2.41	2.32	2.24	2.16
191	3.13	2.99	2.85	2.73	2.62	2.52	2.43	2.34	2.26	2.18
192	3.16	3.01	2.88	2.76	2.64	2.54	2.45	2.36	2.27	2.20
193	3.18	3.03	2.90	2.78	2.66	2.56	2.47	2.38	2.29	2.22
194	3.21	3.06	2.92	2.80	2.69	2.58	2.48	2.39	2.31	2.23
195	3.23	3.08	2.95	2.82	2.71	2.60	2.50	2.41	2.33	2.25
196	3.26	3.11	2.97	2.84	2.73	2.62	2.52	2.43	2.35	2.27
197	3.28	3.13	2.99	2.87	2.75	2.64	2.54	2.45	2.37	2.29
198	3.31	3.15	3.01	2.89	2.77	2.66	2.56	2.47	2.38	2.30
199	3.33	3.18	3.04	2.91	2.79	2.68	2.58	2.49	2.40	2.32
200	3.36	3.20	3.06	2.93	2.81	2.70	2.60	2.51	2.42	2.34

For notes on how to use the table see page 10

TABLE 1. RATES OF GROWTH (COMPOUNDING EACH PERIOD)

NUMBER OF PERIODS

FINAL AMOUNT	31	32	33	34	35	36	37	38	39	40
151	1.34	1.30	1.26	1.22	1.18	1.15	1.12	1.09	1.06	1.04
152	1.36	1.32	1.28	1.24	1.20	1.17	1.14	1.11	1.08	1.05
153	1.38	1.34	1.30	1.26	1.22	1.19	1.16	1.13	1.10	1.07
154	1.40	1.36	1.32	1.28	1.24	1.21	1.17	1.14	1.11	1.09
155	1.42	1.38	1.34	1.30	1.26	1.22	1.19	1.16	1.13	1.10
156	1.44	1.40	1.36	1.32	1.28	1.24	1.21	1.18	1.15	1.12
157	1.47	1.42	1.38	1.34	1.30	1.26	1.23	1.19	1.16	1.13
158	1.49	1.44	1.40	1.35	1.32	1.28	1.24	1.21	1.18	1.15
159	1.51	1.46	1.42	1.37	1.33	1.30	1.26	1.23	1.20	1.17
160	1.53	1.48	1.43	1.39	1.35	1.31	1.28	1.24	1.21	1.18
161	1.55	1.50	1.45	1.41	1.37	1.33	1.30	1.26	1.23	1.20
162	1.57	1.52	1.47	1.43	1.39	1.35	1.31	1.28	1.24	1.21
163	1.59	1.54	1.49	1.45	1.41	1.37	1.33	1.29	1.26	1.23
164	1.61	1.56	1.51	1.47	1.42	1.38	1.35	1.31	1.28	1.24
165	1.63	1.58	1.53	1.48	1.44	1.40	1.36	1.33	1.29	1.26
166	1.65	1.60	1.55	1.50	1.46	1.42	1.38	1.34	1.31	1.28
167	1.67	1.62	1.57	1.52	1.48	1.43	1.40	1.36	1.32	1.29
168	1.69	1.63	1.58	1.54	1.49	1.45	1.41	1.37	1.34	1.31
169	1.71	1.65	1.60	1.56	1.51	1.47	1.43	1.39	1.35	1.32
170	1.73	1.67	1.62	1.57	1.53	1.48	1.44	1.41	1.37	1.34
171	1.75	1.69	1.64	1.59	1.54	1.50	1.46	1.42	1.39	1.35
172	1.76	1.71	1.66	1.61	1.56	1.52	1.48	1.44	1.40	1.37
173	1.78	1.73	1.67	1.63	1.58	1.53	1.49	1.45	1.42	1.38
174	1.80	1.75	1.69	1.64	1.60	1.55	1.51	1.47	1.43	1.39
175	1.82	1.76	1.71	1.66	1.61	1.57	1.52	1.48	1.45	1.41
176	1.84	1.78	1.73	1.68	1.63	1.58	1.54	1.50	1.46	1.42
177	1.86	1.80	1.75	1.69	1.64	1.60	1.56	1.51	1.47	1.44
178	1.88	1.82	1.76	1.71	1.66	1.61	1.57	1.53	1.49	1.45
179	1.90	1.84	1.78	1.73	1.68	1.63	1.59	1.54	1.50	1.47
180	1.91	1.85	1.80	1.74	1.69	1.65	1.60	1.56	1.52	1.48
181	1.93	1.87	1.81	1.76	1.71	1.66	1.62	1.57	1.53	1.49
182	1.95	1.89	1.83	1.78	1.73	1.68	1.63	1.59	1.55	1.51
183	1.97	1.91	1.85	1.79	1.74	1.69	1.65	1.60	1.56	1.52
184	1.99	1.92	1.86	1.81	1.76	1.71	1.66	1.62	1.58	1.54
185	2.00	1.94	1.88	1.83	1.77	1.72	1.68	1.63	1.59	1.55
186	2.02	1.96	1.90	1.84	1.79	1.74	1.69	1.65	1.60	1.56
187	2.04	1.98	1.91	1.86	1.80	1.75	1.71	1.66	1.62	1.58
188	2.06	1.99	1.93	1.87	1.82	1.77	1.72	1.68	1.63	1.59
189	2.07	2.01	1.95	1.89	1.84	1.78	1.74	1.69	1.65	1.60
190	2.09	2.03	1.96	1.91	1.85	1.80	1.75	1.70	1.66	1.62
191	2.11	2.04	1.98	1.92	1.87	1.81	1.76	1.72	1.67	1.63
192	2.13	2.06	2.00	1.94	1.88	1.83	1.78	1.73	1.69	1.64
193	2.14	2.08	2.01	1.95	1.90	1.84	1.79	1.75	1.70	1.66
194	2.16	2.09	2.03	1.97	1.91	1.86	1.81	1.76	1.71	1.67
195	2.18	2.11	2.04	1.98	1.93	1.87	1.82	1.77	1.73	1.68
196	2.19	2.13	2.06	2.00	1.94	1.89	1.84	1.79	1.74	1.70
197	2.21	2.14	2.08	2.01	1.96	1.90	1.85	1.80	1.75	1.71
198	2.23	2.16	2.09	2.03	1.97	1.92	1.86	1.81	1.77	1.72
199	2.24	2.17	2.11	2.04	1.99	1.93	1.88	1.83	1.78	1.74
200	2.26	2.19	2.12	2.06	2.00	1.94	1.89	1.84	1.79	1.75

For notes on how to use the table see page 10

TABLE 1.   RATES OF GROWTH   (COMPOUNDING EACH PERIOD)

NUMBER OF PERIODS

FINAL AMOUNT	41	42	43	44	45	46	47	48	49	50
151	1.01	0.99	0.96	0.94	0.92	0.90	0.88	0.86	0.84	0.83
152	1.03	1.00	0.98	0.96	0.93	0.91	0.89	0.88	0.86	0.84
153	1.04	1.02	0.99	0.97	0.95	0.93	0.91	0.89	0.87	0.85
154	1.06	1.03	1.01	0.99	0.96	0.94	0.92	0.90	0.89	0.87
155	1.07	1.05	1.02	1.00	0.98	0.96	0.94	0.92	0.90	0.88
156	1.09	1.06	1.04	1.02	0.99	0.97	0.95	0.93	0.91	0.89
157	1.11	1.08	1.05	1.03	1.01	0.99	0.96	0.94	0.92	0.91
158	1.12	1.10	1.07	1.05	1.02	1.00	0.98	0.96	0.94	0.92
159	1.14	1.11	1.08	1.06	1.04	1.01	0.99	0.97	0.95	0.93
160	1.15	1.13	1.10	1.07	1.05	1.03	1.01	0.98	0.96	0.94
161	1.17	1.14	1.11	1.09	1.06	1.04	1.02	1.00	0.98	0.96
162	1.18	1.16	1.13	1.10	1.08	1.05	1.03	1.01	0.99	0.97
163	1.20	1.17	1.14	1.12	1.09	1.07	1.04	1.02	1.00	0.98
164	1.21	1.18	1.16	1.13	1.11	1.08	1.06	1.04	1.01	0.99
165	1.23	1.20	1.17	1.14	1.12	1.09	1.07	1.05	1.03	1.01
166	1.24	1.21	1.19	1.16	1.13	1.11	1.08	1.06	1.04	1.02
167	1.26	1.23	1.20	1.17	1.15	1.12	1.10	1.07	1.05	1.03
168	1.27	1.24	1.21	1.19	1.16	1.13	1.11	1.09	1.06	1.04
169	1.29	1.26	1.23	1.20	1.17	1.15	1.12	1.10	1.08	1.05
170	1.30	1.27	1.24	1.21	1.19	1.16	1.14	1.11	1.09	1.07
171	1.32	1.29	1.26	1.23	1.20	1.17	1.15	1.12	1.10	1.08
172	1.33	1.30	1.27	1.24	1.21	1.19	1.16	1.14	1.11	1.09
173	1.35	1.31	1.28	1.25	1.23	1.20	1.17	1.15	1.12	1.10
174	1.36	1.33	1.30	1.27	1.24	1.21	1.19	1.16	1.14	1.11
175	1.37	1.34	1.31	1.28	1.25	1.22	1.20	1.17	1.15	1.13
176	1.39	1.36	1.32	1.29	1.26	1.24	1.21	1.18	1.16	1.14
177	1.40	1.37	1.34	1.31	1.28	1.25	1.22	1.20	1.17	1.15
178	1.42	1.38	1.35	1.32	1.29	1.26	1.23	1.21	1.18	1.16
179	1.43	1.40	1.36	1.33	1.30	1.27	1.25	1.22	1.20	1.17
180	1.44	1.41	1.38	1.34	1.31	1.29	1.26	1.23	1.21	1.18
181	1.46	1.42	1.39	1.36	1.33	1.30	1.27	1.24	1.22	1.19
182	1.47	1.44	1.40	1.37	1.34	1.31	1.28	1.26	1.23	1.20
183	1.48	1.45	1.42	1.38	1.35	1.32	1.29	1.27	1.24	1.22
184	1.50	1.46	1.43	1.40	1.36	1.33	1.31	1.28	1.25	1.23
185	1.51	1.48	1.44	1.41	1.38	1.35	1.32	1.29	1.26	1.24
186	1.53	1.49	1.45	1.42	1.39	1.36	1.33	1.30	1.27	1.25
187	1.54	1.50	1.47	1.43	1.40	1.37	1.34	1.31	1.29	1.26
188	1.55	1.51	1.48	1.45	1.41	1.38	1.35	1.32	1.30	1.27
189	1.56	1.53	1.49	1.46	1.42	1.39	1.36	1.34	1.31	1.28
190	1.58	1.54	1.50	1.47	1.44	1.41	1.38	1.35	1.32	1.29
191	1.59	1.55	1.52	1.48	1.45	1.42	1.39	1.36	1.33	1.30
192	1.60	1.57	1.53	1.49	1.46	1.43	1.40	1.37	1.34	1.31
193	1.62	1.58	1.54	1.51	1.47	1.44	1.41	1.38	1.35	1.32
194	1.63	1.59	1.55	1.52	1.48	1.45	1.42	1.39	1.36	1.33
195	1.64	1.60	1.57	1.53	1.50	1.46	1.43	1.40	1.37	1.34
196	1.65	1.62	1.58	1.54	1.51	1.47	1.44	1.41	1.38	1.35
197	1.67	1.63	1.59	1.55	1.52	1.48	1.45	1.42	1.39	1.37
198	1.68	1.64	1.60	1.56	1.53	1.50	1.46	1.43	1.40	1.38
199	1.69	1.65	1.61	1.58	1.54	1.51	1.47	1.44	1.41	1.39
200	1.70	1.66	1.63	1.59	1.55	1.52	1.49	1.45	1.42	1.40

For notes on how to use the table see page 10

TABLE 1.   RATES OF GROWTH   (COMPOUNDING EACH PERIOD)

NUMBER OF PERIODS

FINAL AMOUNT	60	70	80	90	100	120	140	160	180	200
151	0.69	0.59	0.52	0.46	0.41	0.34	0.29	0.26	0.23	0.21
152	0.70	0.60	0.52	0.47	0.42	0.35	0.30	0.26	0.23	0.21
153	0.71	0.61	0.53	0.47	0.43	0.36	0.30	0.27	0.24	0.21
154	0.72	0.62	0.54	0.48	0.43	0.36	0.31	0.27	0.24	0.22
155	0.73	0.63	0.55	0.49	0.44	0.37	0.31	0.27	0.24	0.22
156	0.74	0.64	0.56	0.50	0.45	0.37	0.32	0.28	0.25	0.22
157	0.75	0.65	0.57	0.50	0.45	0.38	0.32	0.28	0.25	0.23
158	0.77	0.66	0.57	0.51	0.46	0.38	0.33	0.29	0.25	0.23
159	0.78	0.66	0.58	0.52	0.46	0.39	0.33	0.29	0.26	0.23
160	0.79	0.67	0.59	0.52	0.47	0.39	0.34	0.29	0.26	0.24
161	0.80	0.68	0.60	0.53	0.48	0.40	0.34	0.30	0.26	0.24
162	0.81	0.69	0.60	0.54	0.48	0.40	0.35	0.30	0.27	0.24
163	0.82	0.70	0.61	0.54	0.49	0.41	0.35	0.31	0.27	0.24
164	0.83	0.71	0.62	0.55	0.50	0.41	0.35	0.31	0.28	0.25
165	0.84	0.72	0.63	0.56	0.50	0.42	0.36	0.31	0.28	0.25
166	0.85	0.73	0.64	0.56	0.51	0.42	0.36	0.32	0.28	0.25
167	0.86	0.74	0.64	0.57	0.51	0.43	0.37	0.32	0.29	0.26
168	0.87	0.74	0.65	0.58	0.52	0.43	0.37	0.32	0.29	0.26
169	0.88	0.75	0.66	0.58	0.53	0.44	0.38	0.33	0.29	0.26
170	0.89	0.76	0.67	0.59	0.53	0.44	0.38	0.33	0.30	0.27
171	0.90	0.77	0.67	0.60	0.54	0.45	0.38	0.34	0.30	0.27
172	0.91	0.78	0.68	0.60	0.54	0.45	0.39	0.34	0.30	0.27
173	0.92	0.79	0.69	0.61	0.55	0.46	0.39	0.34	0.30	0.27
174	0.93	0.79	0.69	0.62	0.56	0.46	0.40	0.35	0.31	0.28
175	0.94	0.80	0.70	0.62	0.56	0.47	0.40	0.35	0.31	0.28
176	0.95	0.81	0.71	0.63	0.57	0.47	0.40	0.35	0.31	0.28
177	0.96	0.82	0.72	0.64	0.57	0.48	0.41	0.36	0.32	0.29
178	0.97	0.83	0.72	0.64	0.58	0.48	0.41	0.36	0.32	0.29
179	0.98	0.84	0.73	0.65	0.58	0.49	0.42	0.36	0.32	0.29
180	0.98	0.84	0.74	0.66	0.59	0.49	0.42	0.37	0.33	0.29
181	0.99	0.85	0.74	0.66	0.60	0.50	0.42	0.37	0.33	0.30
182	1.00	0.86	0.75	0.67	0.60	0.50	0.43	0.37	0.33	0.30
183	1.01	0.87	0.76	0.67	0.61	0.50	0.43	0.38	0.34	0.30
184	1.02	0.87	0.77	0.68	0.61	0.51	0.44	0.38	0.34	0.31
185	1.03	0.88	0.77	0.69	0.62	0.51	0.44	0.39	0.34	0.31
186	1.04	0.89	0.78	0.69	0.62	0.52	0.44	0.39	0.35	0.31
187	1.05	0.90	0.79	0.70	0.63	0.52	0.45	0.39	0.35	0.31
188	1.06	0.91	0.79	0.70	0.63	0.53	0.45	0.40	0.35	0.32
189	1.07	0.91	0.80	0.71	0.64	0.53	0.46	0.40	0.35	0.32
190	1.08	0.92	0.81	0.72	0.64	0.54	0.46	0.40	0.36	0.32
191	1.08	0.93	0.81	0.72	0.65	0.54	0.46	0.41	0.36	0.32
192	1.09	0.94	0.82	0.73	0.65	0.55	0.47	0.41	0.36	0.33
193	1.10	0.94	0.83	0.73	0.66	0.55	0.47	0.41	0.37	0.33
194	1.11	0.95	0.83	0.74	0.66	0.55	0.47	0.42	0.37	0.33
195	1.12	0.96	0.84	0.74	0.67	0.56	0.48	0.42	0.37	0.33
196	1.13	0.97	0.84	0.75	0.68	0.56	0.48	0.42	0.37	0.34
197	1.14	0.97	0.85	0.76	0.68	0.57	0.49	0.42	0.38	0.34
198	1.15	0.98	0.86	0.76	0.69	0.57	0.49	0.43	0.38	0.34
199	1.15	0.99	0.86	0.77	0.69	0.58	0.49	0.43	0.38	0.34
200	1.16	1.00	0.87	0.77	0.70	0.58	0.50	0.43	0.39	0.35

For notes on how to use the table see page 10

TABLE 1. RATES OF GROWTH (COMPOUNDING EACH PERIOD)

NUMBER OF PERIODS

FINAL AMOUNT	1	2	3	4	5	6	7	8	9	10
202		42.13	26.41	19.22	15.10	12.43	10.57	9.19	8.13	7.28
204		42.83	26.83	19.51	15.33	12.62	10.72	9.32	8.24	7.39
206		43.53	27.24	19.80	15.55	12.80	10.88	9.45	8.36	7.49
208		44.22	27.65	20.09	15.77	12.98	11.03	9.59	8.48	7.60
210		44.91	28.06	20.38	16.00	13.16	11.18	9.72	8.59	7.70
212		45.60	28.46	20.67	16.22	13.34	11.33	9.85	8.71	7.80
214		46.29	28.87	20.95	16.43	13.52	11.48	9.98	8.82	7.90
216		46.97	29.27	21.23	16.65	13.70	11.63	10.10	8.93	8.01
218		47.65	29.66	21.51	16.87	13.87	11.78	10.23	9.05	8.10
220		48.32	30.06	21.79	17.08	14.04	11.92	10.36	9.16	8.20
222		49.00	30.45	22.06	17.29	14.22	12.07	10.48	9.27	8.30
224		49.67	30.84	22.34	17.50	14.39	12.21	10.61	9.37	8.40
226		50.33	31.23	22.61	17.71	14.56	12.35	10.73	9.48	8.50
228		51.00	31.62	22.88	17.92	14.72	12.50	10.85	9.59	8.59
230		51.66	32.00	23.15	18.13	14.89	12.64	10.97	9.70	8.69
232		52.32	32.38	23.42	18.33	15.06	12.77	11.09	9.80	8.78
234		52.97	32.76	23.68	18.53	15.22	12.91	11.21	9.91	8.87
236		53.62	33.14	23.94	18.74	15.39	13.05	11.33	10.01	8.97
238		54.27	33.51	24.21	18.94	15.55	13.19	11.45	10.11	9.06
240		54.92	33.89	24.47	19.14	15.71	13.32	11.56	10.22	9.15
242		55.56	34.26	24.73	19.33	15.87	13.46	11.68	10.32	9.24
244		56.20	34.63	24.98	19.53	16.03	13.59	11.80	10.42	9.33
246		56.84	34.99	25.24	19.73	16.19	13.72	11.91	10.52	9.42
248		57.48	35.36	25.49	19.92	16.34	13.85	12.02	10.62	9.51
250		58.11	35.72	25.74	20.11	16.50	13.99	12.14	10.72	9.60
252		58.75	36.08	25.99	20.30	16.65	14.12	12.25	10.82	9.68
254		59.37	36.44	26.24	20.49	16.81	14.24	12.36	10.91	9.77
256		60.00	36.80	26.49	20.68	16.96	14.37	12.47	11.01	9.86
258		60.62	37.15	26.74	20.87	17.11	14.50	12.58	11.11	9.94
260		61.25	37.51	26.98	21.06	17.26	14.63	12.69	11.20	10.03
262		61.86	37.86	27.23	21.24	17.41	14.75	12.79	11.30	10.11
264		62.48	38.21	27.47	21.43	17.56	14.88	12.90	11.39	10.19
266		63.10	38.56	27.71	21.61	17.71	15.00	13.01	11.48	10.28
268		63.71	38.90	27.95	21.79	17.86	15.12	13.11	11.58	10.36
270		64.32	39.25	28.19	21.98	18.00	15.25	13.22	11.67	10.44
272		64.92	39.59	28.42	22.16	18.15	15.37	13.32	11.76	10.52
274		65.53	39.93	28.66	22.33	18.29	15.49	13.43	11.85	10.61
276		66.13	40.27	28.89	22.51	18.44	15.61	13.53	11.94	10.69
278		66.73	40.61	29.13	22.69	18.58	15.73	13.63	12.03	10.77
280		67.33	40.95	29.36	22.87	18.72	15.85	13.74	12.12	10.84
282		67.93	41.28	29.59	23.04	18.86	15.96	13.84	12.21	10.92
284		68.52	41.61	29.82	23.22	19.00	16.08	13.94	12.30	11.00
286		69.12	41.95	30.04	23.39	19.14	16.20	14.04	12.38	11.08
288		69.71	42.28	30.27	23.56	19.28	16.31	14.14	12.47	11.16
290		70.29	42.60	30.50	23.73	19.42	16.43	14.24	12.56	11.23
292		70.88	42.93	30.72	23.90	19.55	16.54	14.33	12.64	11.31
294		71.46	43.26	30.94	24.07	19.69	16.66	14.43	12.73	11.39
296		72.05	43.58	31.17	24.24	19.83	16.77	14.53	12.81	11.46
298		72.63	43.90	31.39	24.41	19.96	16.88	14.62	12.90	11.54
300		73.21	44.22	31.61	24.57	20.09	16.99	14.72	12.98	11.61

For notes on how to use the table see page 10

TABLE 1. RATES OF GROWTH (COMPOUNDING EACH PERIOD)

NUMBER OF PERIODS

FINAL AMOUNT	11	12	13	14	15	16	17	18	19	20
202	6.60	6.03	5.56	5.15	4.80	4.49	4.22	3.98	3.77	3.58
204	6.70	6.12	5.64	5.22	4.87	4.56	4.28	4.04	3.82	3.63
206	6.79	6.21	5.72	5.30	4.94	4.62	4.34	4.10	3.88	3.68
208	6.88	6.29	5.80	5.37	5.00	4.68	4.40	4.15	3.93	3.73
210	6.98	6.38	5.87	5.44	5.07	4.75	4.46	4.21	3.98	3.78
212	7.07	6.46	5.95	5.51	5.14	4.81	4.52	4.26	4.03	3.83
214	7.16	6.55	6.03	5.58	5.20	4.87	4.58	4.32	4.09	3.88
216	7.25	6.63	6.10	5.65	5.27	4.93	4.63	4.37	4.14	3.93
218	7.34	6.71	6.18	5.72	5.33	4.99	4.69	4.42	4.19	3.97
220	7.43	6.79	6.25	5.79	5.40	5.05	4.75	4.48	4.24	4.02
222	7.52	6.87	6.33	5.86	5.46	5.11	4.80	4.53	4.29	4.07
224	7.61	6.95	6.40	5.93	5.52	5.17	4.86	4.58	4.34	4.11
226	7.69	7.03	6.47	6.00	5.59	5.23	4.91	4.63	4.38	4.16
228	7.78	7.11	6.55	6.06	5.65	5.29	4.97	4.69	4.43	4.21
230	7.87	7.19	6.62	6.13	5.71	5.34	5.02	4.74	4.48	4.25
232	7.95	7.26	6.69	6.20	5.77	5.40	5.07	4.79	4.53	4.30
234	8.04	7.34	6.76	6.26	5.83	5.46	5.13	4.84	4.58	4.34
236	8.12	7.42	6.83	6.33	5.89	5.51	5.18	4.89	4.62	4.39
238	8.20	7.49	6.90	6.39	5.95	5.57	5.23	4.94	4.67	4.43
240	8.28	7.57	6.97	6.45	6.01	5.62	5.28	4.98	4.72	4.47
242	8.37	7.64	7.03	6.52	6.07	5.68	5.34	5.03	4.76	4.52
244	8.45	7.72	7.10	6.58	6.13	5.73	5.39	5.08	4.81	4.56
246	8.53	7.79	7.17	6.64	6.18	5.79	5.44	5.13	4.85	4.60
248	8.61	7.86	7.24	6.70	6.24	5.84	5.49	5.18	4.90	4.65
250	8.69	7.93	7.30	6.76	6.30	5.89	5.54	5.22	4.94	4.69
252	8.77	8.01	7.37	6.82	6.36	5.95	5.59	5.27	4.98	4.73
254	8.84	8.08	7.43	6.88	6.41	6.00	5.64	5.32	5.03	4.77
256	8.92	8.15	7.50	6.94	6.47	6.05	5.69	5.36	5.07	4.81
258	9.00	8.22	7.56	7.00	6.52	6.10	5.73	5.41	5.11	4.85
260	9.07	8.29	7.63	7.06	6.58	6.15	5.78	5.45	5.16	4.89
262	9.15	8.36	7.69	7.12	6.63	6.20	5.83	5.50	5.20	4.93
264	9.23	8.43	7.75	7.18	6.69	6.26	5.88	5.54	5.24	4.97
266	9.30	8.49	7.82	7.24	6.74	6.31	5.92	5.59	5.28	5.01
268	9.38	8.56	7.88	7.30	6.79	6.36	5.97	5.63	5.33	5.05
270	9.45	8.63	7.94	7.35	6.85	6.40	6.02	5.67	5.37	5.09
272	9.52	8.70	8.00	7.41	6.90	6.45	6.06	5.72	5.41	5.13
274	9.60	8.76	8.06	7.47	6.95	6.50	6.11	5.76	5.45	5.17
276	9.67	8.83	8.12	7.52	7.00	6.55	6.15	5.80	5.49	5.21
278	9.74	8.89	8.18	7.58	7.05	6.60	6.20	5.84	5.53	5.25
280	9.81	8.96	8.24	7.63	7.11	6.65	6.24	5.89	5.57	5.28
282	9.88	9.02	8.30	7.69	7.16	6.69	6.29	5.93	5.61	5.32
284	9.95	9.09	8.36	7.74	7.21	6.74	6.33	5.97	5.65	5.36
286	10.02	9.15	8.42	7.79	7.26	6.79	6.38	6.01	5.69	5.39
288	10.09	9.22	8.48	7.85	7.31	6.83	6.42	6.05	5.73	5.43
290	10.16	9.28	8.53	7.90	7.36	6.88	6.46	6.09	5.76	5.47
292	10.23	9.34	8.59	7.95	7.41	6.93	6.51	6.13	5.80	5.50
294	10.30	9.40	8.65	8.01	7.45	6.97	6.55	6.17	5.84	5.54
296	10.37	9.46	8.71	8.06	7.50	7.02	6.59	6.21	5.88	5.58
298	10.44	9.53	8.76	8.11	7.55	7.06	6.63	6.25	5.92	5.61
300	10.50	9.59	8.82	8.16	7.60	7.11	6.68	6.29	5.95	5.65

For notes on how to use the table see page 10

TABLE 1. RATES OF GROWTH (COMPOUNDING EACH PERIOD)

NUMBER OF PERIODS

FINAL AMOUNT	21	22	23	24	25	26	27	28	29	30
202	3.40	3.25	3.10	2.97	2.85	2.74	2.64	2.54	2.45	2.37
204	3.45	3.29	3.15	3.02	2.89	2.78	2.68	2.58	2.49	2.40
206	3.50	3.34	3.19	3.06	2.93	2.82	2.71	2.61	2.52	2.44
208	3.55	3.38	3.24	3.10	2.97	2.86	2.75	2.65	2.56	2.47
210	3.60	3.43	3.28	3.14	3.01	2.89	2.79	2.69	2.59	2.50
212	3.64	3.47	3.32	3.18	3.05	2.93	2.82	2.72	2.62	2.54
214	3.69	3.52	3.36	3.22	3.09	2.97	2.86	2.75	2.66	2.57
216	3.74	3.56	3.40	3.26	3.13	3.01	2.89	2.79	2.69	2.60
218	3.78	3.61	3.45	3.30	3.17	3.04	2.93	2.82	2.72	2.63
220	3.83	3.65	3.49	3.34	3.20	3.08	2.96	2.86	2.76	2.66
222	3.87	3.69	3.53	3.38	3.24	3.11	3.00	2.89	2.79	2.69
224	3.92	3.73	3.57	3.42	3.28	3.15	3.03	2.92	2.82	2.72
226	3.96	3.78	3.61	3.46	3.32	3.19	3.07	2.95	2.85	2.76
228	4.00	3.82	3.65	3.49	3.35	3.22	3.10	2.99	2.88	2.79
230	4.05	3.86	3.69	3.53	3.39	3.26	3.13	3.02	2.91	2.82
232	4.09	3.90	3.73	3.57	3.42	3.29	3.17	3.05	2.94	2.84
234	4.13	3.94	3.77	3.61	3.46	3.32	3.20	3.08	2.97	2.87
236	4.17	3.98	3.80	3.64	3.49	3.36	3.23	3.11	3.01	2.90
238	4.22	4.02	3.84	3.68	3.53	3.39	3.26	3.15	3.04	2.93
240	4.26	4.06	3.88	3.72	3.56	3.42	3.30	3.18	3.06	2.96
242	4.30	4.10	3.92	3.75	3.60	3.46	3.33	3.21	3.09	2.99
244	4.34	4.14	3.95	3.79	3.63	3.49	3.36	3.24	3.12	3.02
246	4.38	4.18	3.99	3.82	3.67	3.52	3.39	3.27	3.15	3.05
248	4.42	4.21	4.03	3.86	3.70	3.56	3.42	3.30	3.18	3.07
250	4.46	4.25	4.06	3.89	3.73	3.59	3.45	3.33	3.21	3.10
252	4.50	4.29	4.10	3.93	3.77	3.62	3.48	3.36	3.24	3.13
254	4.54	4.33	4.14	3.96	3.80	3.65	3.51	3.39	3.27	3.16
256	4.58	4.37	4.17	3.99	3.83	3.68	3.54	3.41	3.29	3.18
258	4.62	4.40	4.21	4.03	3.86	3.71	3.57	3.44	3.32	3.21
260	4.66	4.44	4.24	4.06	3.90	3.74	3.60	3.47	3.35	3.24
262	4.69	4.48	4.28	4.09	3.93	3.77	3.63	3.50	3.38	3.26
264	4.73	4.51	4.31	4.13	3.96	3.80	3.66	3.53	3.40	3.29
266	4.77	4.55	4.35	4.16	3.99	3.83	3.69	3.56	3.43	3.31
268	4.81	4.58	4.38	4.19	4.02	3.86	3.72	3.58	3.46	3.34
270	4.04	4.62	4.41	4.23	4.05	3.89	3.75	3.61	3.48	3.37
272	4.88	4.05	4.45	4.26	4.08	3.92	3.78	3.64	3.51	3.39
274	4.92	4.69	4.48	4.29	4.11	3.95	3.80	3.67	3.54	3.42
276	4.95	4.72	4.51	4.32	4.14	3.98	3.83	3.69	3.56	3.44
278	4.99	4.76	4.55	4.35	4.17	4.01	3.86	3.72	3.59	3.47
280	5.03	4.79	4.58	4.38	4.20	4.04	3.89	3.75	3.61	3.49
282	5.06	4.83	4.61	4.41	4.23	4.07	3.91	3.77	3.64	3.52
284	5.10	4.86	4.64	4.45	4.26	4.10	3.94	3.80	3.66	3.54
286	5.13	4.89	4.67	4.48	4.29	4.12	3.97	3.82	3.69	3.56
288	5.17	4.93	4.71	4.51	4.32	4.15	4.00	3.85	3.71	3.59
290	5.20	4.96	4.74	4.54	4.35	4.18	4.02	3.88	3.74	3.61
292	5.24	4.99	4.77	4.57	4.38	4.21	4.05	3.90	3.76	3.64
294	5.27	5.02	4.80	4.60	4.41	4.23	4.07	3.93	3.79	3.66
296	5.30	5.06	4.83	4.63	4.44	4.26	4.10	3.95	3.81	3.68
298	5.34	5.09	4.86	4.65	4.46	4.29	4.13	3.98	3.84	3.71
300	5.37	5.12	4.89	4.68	4.49	4.32	4.15	4.00	3.86	3.73

For notes on how to use the table see page 10

TABLE 1. RATES OF GROWTH (COMPOUNDING EACH PERIOD)

NUMBER OF PERIODS

FINAL AMOUNT	31	32	33	34	35	36	37	38	39	40
202	2.29	2.22	2.15	2.09	2.03	1.97	1.92	1.87	1.82	1.77
204	2.33	2.25	2.18	2.12	2.06	2.00	1.95	1.89	1.84	1.80
206	2.36	2.28	2.21	2.15	2.09	2.03	1.97	1.92	1.87	1.82
208	2.39	2.32	2.24	2.18	2.11	2.06	2.00	1.95	1.90	1.85
210	2.42	2.35	2.27	2.21	2.14	2.08	2.03	1.97	1.92	1.87
212	2.45	2.38	2.30	2.23	2.17	2.11	2.05	2.00	1.95	1.90
214	2.48	2.41	2.33	2.26	2.20	2.14	2.08	2.02	1.97	1.92
216	2.52	2.44	2.36	2.29	2.22	2.16	2.10	2.05	1.99	1.94
218	2.55	2.47	2.39	2.32	2.25	2.19	2.13	2.07	2.02	1.97
220	2.58	2.49	2.42	2.35	2.28	2.21	2.15	2.10	2.04	1.99
222	2.61	2.52	2.45	2.37	2.30	2.24	2.18	2.12	2.07	2.01
224	2.64	2.55	2.47	2.40	2.33	2.27	2.20	2.14	2.09	2.04
226	2.67	2.58	2.50	2.43	2.36	2.29	2.23	2.17	2.11	2.06
228	2.69	2.61	2.53	2.45	2.38	2.32	2.25	2.19	2.14	2.08
230	2.72	2.64	2.56	2.48	2.41	2.34	2.28	2.22	2.16	2.10
232	2.75	2.66	2.58	2.51	2.43	2.37	2.30	2.24	2.18	2.13
234	2.78	2.69	2.61	2.53	2.46	2.39	2.32	2.26	2.20	2.15
236	2.81	2.72	2.64	2.56	2.48	2.41	2.35	2.29	2.23	2.17
238	2.84	2.75	2.66	2.58	2.51	2.44	2.37	2.31	2.25	2.19
240	2.86	2.77	2.69	2.61	2.53	2.46	2.39	2.33	2.27	2.21
242	2.89	2.80	2.71	2.63	2.56	2.49	2.42	2.35	2.29	2.23
244	2.92	2.83	2.74	2.66	2.58	2.51	2.44	2.38	2.31	2.26
246	2.95	2.85	2.77	2.68	2.61	2.53	2.46	2.40	2.33	2.28
248	2.97	2.88	2.79	2.71	2.63	2.56	2.49	2.42	2.36	2.30
250	3.00	2.90	2.82	2.73	2.65	2.58	2.51	2.44	2.38	2.32
252	3.03	2.93	2.84	2.76	2.68	2.60	2.53	2.46	2.40	2.34
254	3.05	2.96	2.87	2.78	2.70	2.62	2.55	2.48	2.42	2.36
256	3.08	2.98	2.89	2.80	2.72	2.65	2.57	2.50	2.44	2.38
258	3.10	3.01	2.91	2.83	2.74	2.67	2.59	2.53	2.46	2.40
260	3.13	3.03	2.94	2.85	2.77	2.69	2.62	2.55	2.48	2.42
262	3.16	3.06	2.96	2.87	2.79	2.71	2.64	2.57	2.50	2.44
264	3.18	3.08	2.99	2.90	2.81	2.73	2.66	2.59	2.52	2.46
266	3.21	3.10	3.01	2.92	2.83	2.75	2.68	2.61	2.54	2.48
268	3.23	3.13	3.03	2.94	2.86	2.78	2.70	2.63	2.56	2.50
270	3.26	3.15	3.06	2.96	2.88	2.80	2.72	2.65	2.58	2.51
272	3.28	3.18	3.08	2.99	2.90	2.82	2.74	2.67	2.60	2.53
274	3.30	3.20	3.10	3.01	2.92	2.84	2.76	2.69	2.62	2.55
276	3.33	3.22	3.12	3.03	2.94	2.86	2.78	2.71	2.64	2.57
278	3.35	3.25	3.15	3.05	2.96	2.88	2.80	2.73	2.66	2.59
280	3.38	3.27	3.17	3.07	2.99	2.90	2.82	2.75	2.68	2.61
282	3.40	3.29	3.19	3.10	3.01	2.92	2.84	2.77	2.69	2.63
284	3.42	3.32	3.21	3.12	3.03	2.94	2.86	2.78	2.71	2.64
286	3.45	3.34	3.24	3.14	3.05	2.96	2.88	2.80	2.73	2.66
288	3.47	3.36	3.26	3.16	3.07	2.98	2.90	2.82	2.75	2.68
290	3.49	3.38	3.28	3.18	3.09	3.00	2.92	2.84	2.77	2.70
292	3.52	3.41	3.30	3.20	3.11	3.02	2.94	2.86	2.79	2.72
294	3.54	3.43	3.32	3.22	3.13	3.04	2.96	2.88	2.80	2.73
296	3.56	3.45	3.34	3.24	3.15	3.06	2.98	2.90	2.82	2.75
298	3.59	3.47	3.36	3.26	3.17	3.08	3.00	2.92	2.84	2.77
300	3.61	3.49	3.39	3.28	3.19	3.10	3.01	2.93	2.86	2.78

For notes on how to use the table see page 10

TABLE 1. RATES OF GROWTH (COMPOUNDING EACH PERIOD)

NUMBER OF PERIODS

FINAL AMOUNT	41	42	43	44	45	46	47	48	49	50
202	1.73	1.69	1.65	1.61	1.57	1.54	1.51	1.48	1.45	1.42
204	1.75	1.71	1.67	1.63	1.60	1.56	1.53	1.50	1.47	1.44
206	1.78	1.74	1.69	1.66	1.62	1.58	1.55	1.52	1.49	1.46
208	1.80	1.76	1.72	1.68	1.64	1.60	1.57	1.54	1.51	1.48
210	1.83	1.78	1.74	1.70	1.66	1.63	1.59	1.56	1.53	1.49
212	1.85	1.81	1.76	1.72	1.68	1.65	1.61	1.58	1.55	1.51
214	1.87	1.83	1.79	1.74	1.71	1.67	1.63	1.60	1.56	1.53
216	1.90	1.85	1.81	1.77	1.73	1.69	1.65	1.62	1.58	1.55
218	1.92	1.87	1.83	1.79	1.75	1.71	1.67	1.64	1.60	1.57
220	1.94	1.90	1.85	1.81	1.77	1.73	1.69	1.66	1.62	1.59
222	1.96	1.92	1.87	1.83	1.79	1.75	1.71	1.68	1.64	1.61
224	1.99	1.94	1.89	1.85	1.81	1.77	1.73	1.69	1.66	1.63
226	2.01	1.96	1.91	1.87	1.83	1.79	1.75	1.71	1.68	1.64
228	2.03	1.98	1.94	1.89	1.85	1.81	1.77	1.73	1.70	1.66
230	2.05	2.00	1.96	1.91	1.87	1.83	1.79	1.75	1.71	1.68
232	2.07	2.02	1.98	1.93	1.89	1.85	1.81	1.77	1.73	1.70
234	2.10	2.04	2.00	1.95	1.91	1.87	1.83	1.79	1.75	1.71
236	2.12	2.07	2.02	1.97	1.93	1.88	1.84	1.80	1.77	1.73
238	2.14	2.09	2.04	1.99	1.95	1.90	1.86	1.82	1.79	1.75
240	2.16	2.11	2.06	2.01	1.96	1.92	1.88	1.84	1.80	1.77
242	2.18	2.13	2.08	2.03	1.98	1.94	1.90	1.86	1.82	1.78
244	2.20	2.15	2.10	2.05	2.00	1.96	1.92	1.88	1.84	1.80
246	2.22	2.17	2.12	2.07	2.02	1.98	1.93	1.89	1.85	1.82
248	2.24	2.19	2.13	2.09	2.04	1.99	1.95	1.91	1.87	1.83
250	2.26	2.21	2.15	2.10	2.06	2.01	1.97	1.93	1.89	1.85
252	2.28	2.23	2.17	2.12	2.08	2.03	1.99	1.94	1.90	1.87
254	2.30	2.24	2.19	2.14	2.09	2.05	2.00	1.96	1.92	1.88
256	2.32	2.26	2.21	2.16	2.11	2.06	2.02	1.98	1.94	1.90
258	2.34	2.28	2.23	2.18	2.13	2.08	2.04	1.99	1.95	1.91
260	2.36	2.30	2.25	2.20	2.15	2.10	2.05	2.01	1.97	1.93
262	2.38	2.32	2.27	2.21	2.16	2.12	2.07	2.03	1.99	1.95
264	2.40	2.34	2.28	2.23	2.18	2.13	2.09	2.04	2.00	1.96
266	2.41	2.36	2.30	2.25	2.20	2.15	2.10	2.06	2.02	1.98
268	2.43	2.37	2.32	2.27	2.21	2.17	2.12	2.08	2.03	1.99
270	2.45	2.39	2.34	2.28	2.23	2.18	2.14	2.09	2.05	2.01
272	2.47	2.41	2.35	2.30	2.25	2.20	2.15	2.11	2.06	2.02
274	2.49	2.43	2.37	2.32	2.27	2.22	2.17	2.12	2.08	2.04
276	2.51	2.45	2.39	2.33	2.28	2.23	2.18	2.14	2.09	2.05
278	2.53	2.46	2.41	2.35	2.30	2.25	2.20	2.15	2.11	2.07
280	2.54	2.48	2.42	2.37	2.31	2.26	2.21	2.17	2.12	2.08
282	2.56	2.50	2.44	2.38	2.33	2.28	2.23	2.18	2.14	2.10
284	2.58	2.52	2.46	2.40	2.35	2.30	2.25	2.20	2.15	2.11
286	2.60	2.53	2.47	2.42	2.36	2.31	2.26	2.21	2.17	2.12
288	2.61	2.55	2.49	2.43	2.38	2.33	2.28	2.23	2.18	2.14
290	2.63	2.57	2.51	2.45	2.39	2.34	2.29	2.24	2.20	2.15
292	2.65	2.58	2.52	2.47	2.41	2.36	2.31	2.26	2.21	2.17
294	2.67	2.60	2.54	2.48	2.43	2.37	2.32	2.27	2.23	2.18
296	2.68	2.62	2.56	2.50	2.44	2.39	2.34	2.29	2.24	2.19
298	2.70	2.63	2.57	2.51	2.46	2.40	2.35	2.30	2.25	2.21
300	2.72	2.65	2.59	2.53	2.47	2.42	2.37	2.32	2.27	2.22

For notes on how to use the table see page 10

TABLE 1. RATES OF GROWTH (COMPOUNDING EACH PERIOD)

NUMBER OF PERIODS

FINAL AMOUNT	60	70	80	90	100	120	140	160	180	200
202	1.18	1.01	0.88	0.78	0.71	0.59	0.50	0.44	0.39	0.35
204	1.20	1.02	0.90	0.80	0.72	0.60	0.51	0.45	0.40	0.36
206	1.21	1.04	0.91	0.81	0.73	0.60	0.52	0.45	0.40	0.36
208	1.23	1.05	0.92	0.82	0.74	0.61	0.52	0.46	0.41	0.37
210	1.24	1.07	0.93	0.83	0.74	0.62	0.53	0.46	0.41	0.37
212	1.26	1.08	0.94	0.84	0.75	0.63	0.54	0.47	0.42	0.38
214	1.28	1.09	0.96	0.85	0.76	0.64	0.54	0.48	0.42	0.38
216	1.29	1.11	0.97	0.86	0.77	0.64	0.55	0.48	0.43	0.39
218	1.31	1.12	0.98	0.87	0.78	0.65	0.56	0.49	0.43	0.39
220	1.32	1.13	0.99	0.88	0.79	0.66	0.56	0.49	0.44	0.40
222	1.34	1.15	1.00	0.89	0.80	0.67	0.57	0.50	0.44	0.40
224	1.35	1.16	1.01	0.90	0.81	0.67	0.58	0.51	0.45	0.40
226	1.37	1.17	1.02	0.91	0.82	0.68	0.58	0.51	0.45	0.41
228	1.38	1.18	1.04	0.92	0.83	0.69	0.59	0.52	0.46	0.41
230	1.40	1.20	1.05	0.93	0.84	0.70	0.60	0.52	0.46	0.42
232	1.41	1.21	1.06	0.94	0.85	0.70	0.60	0.53	0.47	0.42
234	1.43	1.22	1.07	0.95	0.85	0.71	0.61	0.53	0.47	0.43
236	1.44	1.23	1.08	0.96	0.86	0.72	0.62	0.54	0.48	0.43
238	1.46	1.25	1.09	0.97	0.87	0.73	0.62	0.54	0.48	0.43
240	1.47	1.26	1.10	0.98	0.88	0.73	0.63	0.55	0.49	0.44
242	1.48	1.27	1.11	0.99	0.89	0.74	0.63	0.55	0.49	0.44
244	1.50	1.28	1.12	1.00	0.90	0.75	0.64	0.56	0.50	0.45
246	1.51	1.29	1.13	1.01	0.90	0.75	0.65	0.56	0.50	0.45
248	1.53	1.31	1.14	1.01	0.91	0.76	0.65	0.57	0.51	0.46
250	1.54	1.32	1.15	1.02	0.92	0.77	0.66	0.57	0.51	0.46
252	1.55	1.33	1.16	1.03	0.93	0.77	0.66	0.58	0.51	0.46
254	1.57	1.34	1.17	1.04	0.94	0.78	0.67	0.58	0.52	0.47
256	1.58	1.35	1.18	1.05	0.94	0.79	0.67	0.59	0.52	0.47
258	1.59	1.36	1.19	1.06	0.95	0.79	0.68	0.59	0.53	0.48
260	1.61	1.37	1.20	1.07	0.96	0.80	0.68	0.60	0.53	0.48
262	1.62	1.39	1.21	1.08	0.97	0.81	0.69	0.60	0.54	0.48
264	1.63	1.40	1.22	1.08	0.98	0.81	0.70	0.61	0.54	0.49
266	1.64	1.41	1.23	1.09	0.98	0.82	0.70	0.61	0.54	0.49
268	1.66	1.42	1.24	1.10	0.99	0.82	0.71	0.62	0.55	0.49
270	1.67	1.43	1.25	1.11	1.00	0.83	0.71	0.62	0.55	0.50
272	1.68	1.44	1.26	1.12	1.01	0.84	0.72	0.63	0.56	0.50
274	1.69	1.45	1.27	1.13	1.01	0.84	0.72	0.63	0.56	0.51
276	1.71	1.46	1.28	1.13	1.02	0.85	0.73	0.64	0.57	0.51
278	1.72	1.47	1.29	1.14	1.03	0.86	0.73	0.64	0.57	0.51
280	1.73	1.48	1.30	1.15	1.03	0.86	0.74	0.65	0.57	0.52
282	1.74	1.49	1.30	1.16	1.04	0.87	0.74	0.65	0.58	0.52
284	1.75	1.50	1.31	1.17	1.05	0.87	0.75	0.65	0.58	0.52
286	1.77	1.51	1.32	1.17	1.06	0.88	0.75	0.66	0.59	0.53
288	1.78	1.52	1.33	1.18	1.06	0.89	0.76	0.66	0.59	0.53
290	1.79	1.53	1.34	1.19	1.07	0.89	0.76	0.67	0.59	0.53
292	1.80	1.54	1.35	1.20	1.08	0.90	0.77	0.67	0.60	0.54
294	1.81	1.55	1.36	1.21	1.08	0.90	0.77	0.68	0.60	0.54
296	1.83	1.56	1.37	1.21	1.09	0.91	0.78	0.68	0.60	0.54
298	1.84	1.57	1.37	1.22	1.10	0.91	0.78	0.68	0.61	0.55
300	1.85	1.58	1.38	1.23	1.10	0.92	0.79	0.69	0.61	0.55

For notes on how to use the table see page 10

TABLE 1. RATES OF GROWTH (COMPOUNDING EACH PERIOD)

NUMBER OF PERIODS

FINAL AMOUNT	1	2	3	4	5	6	7	8	9	10
302	73.78	44.54	31.83	24.74	20.23	17.10	14.82	13.07	11.69	
304	74.36	44.86	32.04	24.90	20.36	17.21	14.91	13.15	11.76	
306	74.93	45.18	32.26	25.07	20.49	17.32	15.00	13.23	11.83	
308	75.50	45.50	32.48	25.23	20.62	17.43	15.10	13.31	11.91	
310	76.07	45.81	32.69	25.39	20.75	17.54	15.19	13.40	11.98	
312	76.64	46.12	32.90	25.55	20.88	17.65	15.28	13.48	12.05	
314	77.20	46.43	33.12	25.71	21.01	17.76	15.38	13.56	12.12	
316	77.76	46.74	33.33	25.87	21.14	17.86	15.47	13.64	12.19	
318	78.33	47.05	33.54	26.03	21.27	17.97	15.56	13.72	12.26	
320	78.89	47.36	33.75	26.19	21.39	18.08	15.65	13.80	12.33	
322	79.44	47.67	33.96	26.35	21.52	18.18	15.74	13.88	12.40	
324	80.00	47.97	34.16	26.51	21.64	18.29	15.83	13.95	12.47	
326	80.55	48.28	34.37	26.66	21.77	18.39	15.92	14.03	12.54	
328	81.11	48.58	34.58	26.82	21.89	18.49	16.01	14.11	12.61	
330	81.66	48.88	34.78	26.97	22.02	18.60	16.10	14.19	12.68	
332	82.21	49.18	34.98	27.12	22.14	18.70	16.18	14.26	12.75	
334	82.76	49.48	35.19	27.28	22.26	18.80	16.27	14.34	12.82	
336	83.30	49.78	35.39	27.43	22.38	18.90	16.36	14.41	12.88	
338	83.85	50.07	35.59	27.58	22.50	19.00	16.44	14.49	12.95	
340	84.39	50.37	35.79	27.73	22.63	19.10	16.53	14.57	13.02	
342	84.93	50.66	35.99	27.88	22.75	19.20	16.61	14.64	13.08	
344	85.47	50.96	36.19	28.03	22.86	19.30	16.70	14.71	13.15	
346	86.01	51.25	36.39	28.18	22.98	19.40	16.78	14.79	13.22	
348	86.55	51.54	36.58	28.33	23.10	19.50	16.87	14.86	13.28	
350	87.08	51.83	36.78	28.47	23.22	19.60	16.95	14.93	13.35	
352	87.62	52.12	36.97	28.62	23.34	19.70	17.04	15.01	13.41	
354	88.15	52.41	37.17	28.77	23.45	19.79	17.12	15.08	13.48	
356	88.68	52.69	37.36	28.91	23.57	19.89	17.20	15.15	13.54	
358	89.21	52.98	37.55	29.06	23.68	19.98	17.28	15.22	13.60	
360	89.74	53.26	37.74	29.20	23.80	20.08	17.36	15.30	13.67	
362	90.26	53.55	37.94	29.34	23.91	20.18	17.45	15.37	13.73	
364	90.79	53.83	38.13	29.49	24.03	20.27	17.53	15.44	13.79	
366	91.31	54.11	38.32	29.63	24.14	20.36	17.61	15.51	13.85	
368	91.83	54.39	38.50	29.77	24.25	20.46	17.69	15.58	13.92	
370	92.35	54.67	38.69	29.91	24.37	20.55	17.77	15.65	13.98	
372	92.87	54.95	38.88	30.05	24.48	20.64	17.85	15.72	14.04	
374	93.39	55.22	39.07	30.19	24.59	20.74	17.93	15.79	14.10	
376	93.91	55.50	39.25	30.33	24.70	20.83	18.00	15.85	14.16	
378	94.42	55.77	39.44	30.47	24.81	20.92	18.08	15.92	14.22	
380	94.94	56.05	39.62	30.60	24.92	21.01	18.16	15.99	14.28	
382	95.45	56.32	39.80	30.74	25.03	21.10	18.24	16.06	14.34	
384	95.96	56.59	39.99	30.88	25.14	21.19	18.32	16.12	14.40	
386	96.47	56.87	40.17	31.01	25.25	21.28	18.39	16.19	14.46	
388	96.98	57.14	40.35	31.15	25.35	21.37	18.47	16.26	14.52	
390	97.48	57.41	40.53	31.28	25.46	21.46	18.54	16.33	14.58	
392	97.99	57.67	40.71	31.42	25.57	21.55	18.62	16.39	14.64	
394	98.49	57.94	40.89	31.55	25.68	21.64	18.70	16.46	14.70	
396	99.00	58.21	41.07	31.69	25.78	21.73	18.77	16.52	14.75	
398	99.50	58.48	41.24	31.82	25.89	21.81	18.85	16.59	14.81	
400		58.74	41.42	31.95	25.99	21.90	18.92	16.65	14.87	

For notes on how to use the table see page 10

TABLE 1. RATES OF GROWTH (COMPOUNDING EACH PERIOD)

NUMBER OF PERIODS

FINAL AMOUNT	11	12	13	14	15	16	17	18	19	20
302	10.57	9.65	8.87	8.21	7.65	7.15	6.72	6.33	5.99	5.68
304	10.64	9.71	8.93	8.27	7.69	7.20	6.76	6.37	6.03	5.72
306	10.70	9.77	8.98	8.32	7.74	7.24	6.80	6.41	6.06	5.75
308	10.77	9.83	9.04	8.37	7.79	7.28	6.84	6.45	6.10	5.79
310	10.83	9.89	9.09	8.42	7.83	7.33	6.88	6.49	6.14	5.82
312	10.90	9.95	9.15	8.47	7.88	7.37	6.92	6.53	6.17	5.85
314	10.96	10.00	9.20	8.52	7.93	7.41	6.96	6.56	6.21	5.89
316	11.03	10.06	9.25	8.57	7.97	7.46	7.00	6.60	6.24	5.92
318	11.09	10.12	9.31	8.61	8.02	7.50	7.04	6.64	6.28	5.95
320	11.15	10.18	9.36	8.66	8.06	7.54	7.08	6.68	6.31	5.99
322	11.22	10.24	9.41	8.71	8.11	7.58	7.12	6.71	6.35	6.02
324	11.28	10.29	9.46	8.76	8.15	7.62	7.16	6.75	6.38	6.05
326	11.34	10.35	9.52	8.81	8.20	7.67	7.20	6.79	6.42	6.09
328	11.40	10.41	9.57	8.85	8.24	7.71	7.24	6.82	6.45	6.12
330	11.46	10.46	9.62	8.90	8.28	7.75	7.28	6.86	6.49	6.15
332	11.53	10.52	9.67	8.95	8.33	7.79	7.31	6.89	6.52	6.18
334	11.59	10.57	9.72	9.00	8.37	7.83	7.35	6.93	6.55	6.22
336	11.65	10.63	9.77	9.04	8.41	7.87	7.39	6.96	6.59	6.25
338	11.71	10.68	9.82	9.09	8.46	7.91	7.43	7.00	6.62	6.28
340	11.77	10.74	9.87	9.13	8.50	7.95	7.46	7.04	6.65	6.31
342	11.83	10.79	9.92	9.18	8.54	7.99	7.50	7.07	6.69	6.34
344	11.89	10.84	9.97	9.23	8.59	8.03	7.54	7.10	6.72	6.37
346	11.95	10.90	10.02	9.27	8.63	8.07	7.57	7.14	6.75	6.40
348	12.00	10.95	10.07	9.32	8.67	8.11	7.61	7.17	6.78	6.43
350	12.06	11.00	10.12	9.36	8.71	8.14	7.65	7.21	6.82	6.46
352	12.12	11.06	10.16	9.41	8.75	8.18	7.68	7.24	6.85	6.49
354	12.18	11.11	10.21	9.45	8.79	8.22	7.72	7.28	6.88	6.52
356	12.24	11.16	10.26	9.49	8.83	8.26	7.76	7.31	6.91	6.55
358	12.29	11.21	10.31	9.54	8.87	8.30	7.79	7.34	6.94	6.58
360	12.35	11.26	10.36	9.58	8.91	8.34	7.83	7.38	6.97	6.61
362	12.41	11.32	10.40	9.62	8.96	8.37	7.86	7.41	7.01	6.64
364	12.46	11.37	10.45	9.67	9.00	8.41	7.90	7.44	7.04	6.67
366	12.52	11.42	10.50	9.71	9.03	8.45	7.93	7.47	7.07	6.70
368	12.57	11.47	10.54	9.75	9.07	8.48	7.97	7.51	7.10	6.73
370	12.63	11.52	10.59	9.80	9.11	8.52	8.00	7.54	7.13	6.76
372	12.69	11.57	10.63	9.84	9.15	8.56	8.03	7.57	7.16	6.79
374	12.74	11.62	10.68	9.88	9.19	8.59	8.07	7.60	7.19	6.82
376	12.79	11.67	10.72	9.92	9.23	8.63	8.10	7.64	7.22	6.85
378	12.85	11.72	10.77	9.96	9.27	8.67	8.14	7.67	7.25	6.87
380	12.90	11.77	10.82	10.01	9.31	8.70	8.17	7.70	7.28	6.90
382	12.96	11.82	10.86	10.05	9.35	8.74	8.20	7.73	7.31	6.93
384	13.01	11.87	10.90	10.09	9.38	8.77	8.24	7.76	7.34	6.96
386	13.06	11.91	10.95	10.13	9.42	8.81	8.27	7.79	7.37	6.99
388	13.12	11.96	10.99	10.17	9.46	8.84	8.30	7.82	7.40	7.01
390	13.17	12.01	11.04	10.21	9.50	8.88	8.33	7.85	7.43	7.04
392	13.22	12.06	11.08	10.25	9.53	8.91	8.37	7.88	7.45	7.07
394	13.28	12.10	11.12	10.29	9.57	8.95	8.40	7.92	7.48	7.10
396	13.33	12.15	11.17	10.33	9.61	8.98	8.43	7.95	7.51	7.12
398	13.38	12.20	11.21	10.37	9.65	9.02	8.46	7.98	7.54	7.15
400	13.43	12.25	11.25	10.41	9.68	9.05	8.50	8.01	7.57	7.18

For notes on how to use the table see page 10

TABLE 1. RATES OF GROWTH (COMPOUNDING EACH PERIOD)

NUMBER OF PERIODS

FINAL AMOUNT	21	22	23	24	25	26	27	28	29	30
302	5.40	5.15	4.92	4.71	4.52	4.34	4.18	4.03	3.88	3.75
304	5.44	5.18	4.95	4.74	4.55	4.37	4.20	4.05	3.91	3.78
306	5.47	5.22	4.98	4.77	4.58	4.40	4.23	4.08	3.93	3.80
308	5.50	5.25	5.01	4.80	4.60	4.42	4.25	4.10	3.96	3.82
310	5.54	5.28	5.04	4.83	4.63	4.45	4.28	4.12	3.98	3.84
312	5.57	5.31	5.07	4.86	4.66	4.47	4.30	4.15	4.00	3.87
314	5.60	5.34	5.10	4.88	4.68	4.50	4.33	4.17	4.02	3.89
316	5.63	5.37	5.13	4.91	4.71	4.52	4.35	4.19	4.05	3.91
318	5.66	5.40	5.16	4.94	4.74	4.55	4.38	4.22	4.07	3.93
320	5.70	5.43	5.19	4.97	4.76	4.58	4.40	4.24	4.09	3.95
322	5.73	5.46	5.22	4.99	4.79	4.60	4.43	4.26	4.11	3.97
324	5.76	5.49	5.24	5.02	4.81	4.63	4.45	4.29	4.14	4.00
326	5.79	5.52	5.27	5.05	4.84	4.65	4.47	4.31	4.16	4.02
328	5.82	5.55	5.30	5.07	4.87	4.67	4.50	4.33	4.18	4.04
330	5.85	5.58	5.33	5.10	4.89	4.70	4.52	4.36	4.20	4.06
332	5.88	5.61	5.36	5.13	4.92	4.72	4.54	4.38	4.22	4.08
334	5.91	5.63	5.38	5.15	4.94	4.75	4.57	4.40	4.25	4.10
336	5.94	5.66	5.41	5.18	4.97	4.77	4.59	4.42	4.27	4.12
338	5.97	5.69	5.44	5.21	4.99	4.80	4.61	4.45	4.29	4.14
340	6.00	5.72	5.46	5.23	5.02	4.82	4.64	4.47	4.31	4.16
342	6.03	5.75	5.49	5.26	5.04	4.84	4.66	4.49	4.33	4.18
344	6.06	5.78	5.52	5.28	5.07	4.87	4.68	4.51	4.35	4.20
346	6.09	5.80	5.55	5.31	5.09	4.89	4.70	4.53	4.37	4.22
348	6.12	5.83	5.57	5.33	5.11	4.91	4.73	4.55	4.39	4.24
350	6.15	5.86	5.60	5.36	5.14	4.94	4.75	4.58	4.41	4.26
352	6.18	5.89	5.62	5.38	5.16	4.96	4.77	4.60	4.44	4.28
354	6.20	5.91	5.65	5.41	5.19	4.98	4.79	4.62	4.46	4.30
356	6.23	5.94	5.68	5.43	5.21	5.00	4.82	4.64	4.48	4.32
358	6.26	5.97	5.70	5.46	5.23	5.03	4.84	4.66	4.50	4.34
360	6.29	6.00	5.73	5.48	5.26	5.05	4.86	4.68	4.52	4.36
362	6.32	6.02	5.75	5.51	5.28	5.07	4.88	4.70	4.54	4.38
364	6.35	6.05	5.78	5.53	5.30	5.09	4.90	4.72	4.56	4.40
366	6.37	6.07	5.80	5.55	5.33	5.12	4.92	4.74	4.58	4.42
368	6.40	6.10	5.83	5.58	5.35	5.14	4.94	4.76	4.60	4.44
370	6.43	6.13	5.85	5.60	5.37	5.16	4.96	4.78	4.61	4.46
372	6.46	6.15	5.88	5.63	5.40	5.18	4.99	4.80	4.63	4.48
374	6.48	6.18	5.90	5.65	5.42	5.20	5.01	4.82	4.65	4.50
376	6.51	6.20	5.93	5.67	5.44	5.23	5.03	4.84	4.67	4.51
378	6.54	6.23	5.95	5.70	5.46	5.25	5.05	4.86	4.69	4.53
380	6.56	6.26	5.98	5.72	5.49	5.27	5.07	4.88	4.71	4.55
382	6.59	6.28	6.00	5.74	5.51	5.29	5.09	4.90	4.73	4.57
384	6.62	6.31	6.02	5.77	5.53	5.31	5.11	4.92	4.75	4.59
386	6.64	6.33	6.05	5.79	5.55	5.33	5.13	4.94	4.77	4.61
388	6.67	6.36	6.07	5.81	5.57	5.35	5.15	4.96	4.79	4.62
390	6.70	6.38	6.10	5.83	5.59	5.37	5.17	4.98	4.80	4.64
392	6.72	6.41	6.12	5.86	5.62	5.39	5.19	5.00	4.82	4.66
394	6.75	6.43	6.14	5.88	5.64	5.42	5.21	5.02	4.84	4.68
396	6.77	6.46	6.17	5.90	5.66	5.44	5.23	5.04	4.86	4.69
398	6.80	6.48	6.19	5.92	5.68	5.46	5.25	5.06	4.88	4.71
400	6.82	6.50	6.21	5.95	5.70	5.48	5.27	5.08	4.90	4.73

For notes on how to use the table see page 10

TABLE 1. RATES OF GROWTH (COMPOUNDING EACH PERIOD)

NUMBER OF PERIODS

FINAL AMOUNT	31	32	33	34	35	36	37	38	39	40
302	3.63	3.51	3.41	3.30	3.21	3.12	3.03	2.95	2.87	2.80
304	3.65	3.54	3.43	3.32	3.23	3.14	3.05	2.97	2.89	2.82
306	3.67	3.56	3.45	3.34	3.25	3.16	3.07	2.99	2.91	2.84
308	3.70	3.58	3.47	3.36	3.27	3.17	3.09	3.00	2.93	2.85
310	3.72	3.60	3.49	3.38	3.29	3.19	3.11	3.02	2.94	2.87
312	3.74	3.62	3.51	3.40	3.30	3.21	3.12	3.04	2.96	2.89
314	3.76	3.64	3.53	3.42	3.32	3.23	3.14	3.06	2.98	2.90
316	3.78	3.66	3.55	3.44	3.34	3.25	3.16	3.07	2.99	2.92
318	3.80	3.68	3.57	3.46	3.36	3.27	3.18	3.09	3.01	2.93
320	3.82	3.70	3.59	3.48	3.38	3.28	3.19	3.11	3.03	2.95
322	3.84	3.72	3.61	3.50	3.40	3.30	3.21	3.13	3.04	2.97
324	3.86	3.74	3.63	3.52	3.42	3.32	3.23	3.14	3.06	2.98
326	3.89	3.76	3.65	3.54	3.43	3.34	3.25	3.16	3.08	3.00
328	3.91	3.78	3.67	3.56	3.45	3.35	3.26	3.18	3.09	3.01
330	3.93	3.80	3.68	3.57	3.47	3.37	3.28	3.19	3.11	3.03
332	3.95	3.82	3.70	3.59	3.49	3.39	3.30	3.21	3.12	3.05
334	3.97	3.84	3.72	3.61	3.51	3.41	3.31	3.22	3.14	3.06
336	3.99	3.86	3.74	3.63	3.52	3.42	3.33	3.24	3.16	3.08
338	4.01	3.88	3.76	3.65	3.54	3.44	3.35	3.26	3.17	3.09
340	4.03	3.90	3.78	3.66	3.56	3.46	3.36	3.27	3.19	3.11
342	4.05	3.92	3.80	3.68	3.58	3.47	3.38	3.29	3.20	3.12
344	4.07	3.94	3.81	3.70	3.59	3.49	3.40	3.30	3.22	3.14
346	4.09	3.96	3.83	3.72	3.61	3.51	3.41	3.32	3.23	3.15
348	4.10	3.97	3.85	3.74	3.63	3.52	3.43	3.34	3.25	3.17
350	4.12	3.99	3.87	3.75	3.64	3.54	3.44	3.35	3.26	3.18
352	4.14	4.01	3.89	3.77	3.66	3.56	3.46	3.37	3.28	3.20
354	4.16	4.03	3.91	3.79	3.68	3.57	3.48	3.38	3.29	3.21
356	4.18	4.05	3.92	3.81	3.69	3.59	3.49	3.40	3.31	3.23
358	4.20	4.07	3.94	3.82	3.71	3.61	3.51	3.41	3.32	3.24
360	4.22	4.08	3.96	3.84	3.73	3.62	3.52	3.43	3.34	3.25
362	4.24	4.10	3.98	3.86	3.74	3.64	3.54	3.44	3.35	3.27
364	4.26	4.12	3.99	3.87	3.76	3.65	3.55	3.46	3.37	3.28
366	4.27	4.14	4.01	3.89	3.78	3.67	3.57	3.47	3.38	3.30
368	4.29	4.16	4.03	3.91	3.79	3.69	3.58	3.49	3.40	3.31
370	4.31	4.17	4.04	3.92	3.81	3.70	3.60	3.50	3.41	3.32
372	4.33	4.19	4.06	3.94	3.82	3.72	3.61	3.52	3.43	3.34
374	4.35	4.21	4.08	3.96	3.84	3.73	3.63	3.53	3.44	3.35
376	4.36	4.23	4.10	3.97	3.86	3.75	3.64	3.55	3.45	3.37
378	4.38	4.24	4.11	3.99	3.87	3.76	3.66	3.56	3.47	3.38
380	4.40	4.26	4.13	4.00	3.89	3.78	3.67	3.58	3.48	3.39
382	4.42	4.28	4.14	4.02	3.90	3.79	3.69	3.59	3.50	3.41
384	4.44	4.29	4.16	4.04	3.92	3.81	3.70	3.60	3.51	3.42
386	4.45	4.31	4.18	4.05	3.93	3.82	3.72	3.62	3.52	3.43
388	4.47	4.33	4.19	4.07	3.95	3.84	3.73	3.63	3.54	3.45
390	4.49	4.34	4.21	4.08	3.97	3.85	3.75	3.65	3.55	3.46
392	4.51	4.36	4.23	4.10	3.98	3.87	3.76	3.66	3.56	3.47
394	4.52	4.38	4.24	4.12	4.00	3.88	3.78	3.67	3.58	3.49
396	4.54	4.39	4.26	4.13	4.01	3.90	3.79	3.69	3.59	3.50
398	4.56	4.41	4.27	4.15	4.03	3.91	3.80	3.70	3.61	3.51
400	4.57	4.43	4.29	4.16	4.04	3.93	3.82	3.72	3.62	3.53

For notes on how to use the table see page 10

TABLE 1.   RATES OF GROWTH   (COMPOUNDING EACH PERIOD)

NUMBER OF PERIODS

FINAL AMOUNT	41	42	43	44	45	46	47	48	49	50
302	2.73	2.67	2.60	2.54	2.49	2.43	2.38	2.33	2.28	2.24
304	2.75	2.68	2.62	2.56	2.50	2.45	2.39	2.34	2.30	2.25
306	2.77	2.70	2.64	2.57	2.52	2.46	2.41	2.36	2.31	2.26
308	2.78	2.71	2.65	2.59	2.53	2.48	2.42	2.37	2.32	2.28
310	2.80	2.73	2.67	2.60	2.55	2.49	2.44	2.39	2.34	2.29
312	2.81	2.75	2.68	2.62	2.56	2.50	2.45	2.40	2.35	2.30
314	2.83	2.76	2.70	2.63	2.58	2.52	2.46	2.41	2.36	2.31
316	2.85	2.78	2.71	2.65	2.59	2.53	2.48	2.43	2.38	2.33
318	2.86	2.79	2.73	2.66	2.60	2.55	2.49	2.44	2.39	2.34
320	2.88	2.81	2.74	2.68	2.62	2.56	2.51	2.45	2.40	2.35
322	2.89	2.82	2.76	2.69	2.63	2.57	2.52	2.47	2.42	2.37
324	2.91	2.84	2.77	2.71	2.65	2.59	2.53	2.48	2.43	2.38
326	2.92	2.85	2.79	2.72	2.66	2.60	2.55	2.49	2.44	2.39
328	2.94	2.87	2.80	2.74	2.67	2.62	2.56	2.51	2.45	2.40
330	2.95	2.88	2.82	2.75	2.69	2.63	2.57	2.52	2.47	2.42
332	2.97	2.90	2.83	2.76	2.70	2.64	2.59	2.53	2.48	2.43
334	2.99	2.91	2.84	2.78	2.72	2.66	2.60	2.54	2.49	2.44
336	3.00	2.93	2.86	2.79	2.73	2.67	2.61	2.56	2.50	2.45
338	3.01	2.94	2.87	2.81	2.74	2.68	2.63	2.57	2.52	2.47
340	3.03	2.96	2.89	2.82	2.76	2.70	2.64	2.58	2.53	2.48
342	3.04	2.97	2.90	2.83	2.77	2.71	2.65	2.59	2.54	2.49
344	3.06	2.99	2.91	2.85	2.78	2.72	2.66	2.61	2.55	2.50
346	3.07	3.00	2.93	2.86	2.80	2.74	2.68	2.62	2.57	2.51
348	3.09	3.01	2.94	2.87	2.81	2.75	2.69	2.63	2.58	2.53
350	3.10	3.03	2.96	2.89	2.82	2.76	2.70	2.64	2.59	2.54
352	3.12	3.04	2.97	2.90	2.84	2.77	2.71	2.66	2.60	2.55
354	3.13	3.06	2.98	2.91	2.85	2.79	2.73	2.67	2.61	2.56
356	3.15	3.07	3.00	2.93	2.86	2.80	2.74	2.68	2.63	2.57
358	3.16	3.08	3.01	2.94	2.87	2.81	2.75	2.69	2.64	2.58
360	3.17	3.10	3.02	2.95	2.89	2.82	2.76	2.70	2.65	2.59
362	3.19	3.11	3.04	2.97	2.90	2.84	2.77	2.72	2.66	2.61
364	3.20	3.12	3.05	2.98	2.91	2.85	2.79	2.73	2.67	2.62
366	3.22	3.14	3.06	2.99	2.93	2.86	2.80	2.74	2.68	2.63
368	3.23	3.15	3.08	3.01	2.94	2.87	2.81	2.75	2.69	2.64
370	3.24	3.16	3.09	3.02	2.95	2.89	2.82	2.76	2.71	2.65
372	3.26	3.18	3.10	3.03	2.96	2.90	2.83	2.77	2.72	2.66
374	3.27	3.19	3.12	3.04	2.97	2.91	2.85	2.79	2.73	2.67
376	3.28	3.20	3.13	3.06	2.99	2.92	2.86	2.80	2.74	2.68
378	3.30	3.22	3.14	3.07	3.00	2.93	2.87	2.81	2.75	2.70
380	3.31	3.23	3.15	3.08	3.01	2.94	2.88	2.82	2.76	2.71
382	3.32	3.24	3.17	3.09	3.02	2.96	2.89	2.83	2.77	2.72
384	3.34	3.26	3.18	3.11	3.04	2.97	2.90	2.84	2.78	2.73
386	3.35	3.27	3.19	3.12	3.05	2.98	2.92	2.85	2.79	2.74
388	3.36	3.28	3.20	3.13	3.06	2.99	2.93	2.86	2.81	2.75
390	3.38	3.29	3.22	3.14	3.07	3.00	2.94	2.88	2.82	2.76
392	3.39	3.31	3.23	3.15	3.08	3.01	2.95	2.89	2.83	2.77
394	3.40	3.32	3.24	3.17	3.09	3.03	2.96	2.90	2.84	2.78
396	3.41	3.33	3.25	3.18	3.11	3.04	2.97	2.91	2.85	2.79
398	3.43	3.34	3.26	3.19	3.12	3.05	2.98	2.92	2.86	2.80
400	3.44	3.36	3.28	3.20	3.13	3.06	2.99	2.93	2.87	2.81

For notes on how to use the table see page 10

TABLE 1. RATES OF GROWTH (COMPOUNDING EACH PERIOD)

NUMBER OF PERIODS

FINAL AMOUNT	60	70	80	90	100	120	140	160	180	200
302	1.86	1.59	1.39	1.24	1.11	0.93	0.79	0.69	0.62	0.55
304	1.87	1.60	1.40	1.24	1.12	0.93	0.80	0.70	0.62	0.56
306	1.88	1.61	1.41	1.25	1.12	0.94	0.80	0.70	0.62	0.56
308	1.89	1.62	1.42	1.26	1.13	0.94	0.81	0.71	0.63	0.56
310	1.90	1.63	1.42	1.27	1.14	0.95	0.81	0.71	0.63	0.57
312	1.91	1.64	1.43	1.27	1.14	0.95	0.82	0.71	0.63	0.57
314	1.93	1.65	1.44	1.28	1.15	0.96	0.82	0.72	0.64	0.57
316	1.94	1.66	1.45	1.29	1.16	0.96	0.83	0.72	0.64	0.58
318	1.95	1.67	1.46	1.29	1.16	0.97	0.83	0.73	0.64	0.58
320	1.96	1.68	1.46	1.30	1.17	0.97	0.83	0.73	0.65	0.58
322	1.97	1.68	1.47	1.31	1.18	0.98	0.84	0.73	0.65	0.59
324	1.98	1.69	1.48	1.31	1.18	0.98	0.84	0.74	0.66	0.59
326	1.99	1.70	1.49	1.32	1.19	0.99	0.85	0.74	0.66	0.59
328	2.00	1.71	1.50	1.33	1.19	0.99	0.85	0.75	0.66	0.60
330	2.01	1.72	1.50	1.34	1.20	1.00	0.86	0.75	0.67	0.60
332	2.02	1.73	1.51	1.34	1.21	1.00	0.86	0.75	0.67	0.60
334	2.03	1.74	1.52	1.35	1.21	1.01	0.87	0.76	0.67	0.60
336	2.04	1.75	1.53	1.36	1.22	1.02	0.87	0.76	0.68	0.61
338	2.05	1.76	1.53	1.36	1.23	1.02	0.87	0.76	0.68	0.61
340	2.06	1.76	1.54	1.37	1.23	1.03	0.88	0.77	0.68	0.61
342	2.07	1.77	1.55	1.38	1.24	1.03	0.88	0.77	0.69	0.62
344	2.08	1.78	1.56	1.38	1.24	1.03	0.89	0.78	0.69	0.62
346	2.09	1.79	1.56	1.39	1.25	1.04	0.89	0.78	0.69	0.62
348	2.10	1.80	1.57	1.40	1.25	1.04	0.89	0.78	0.70	0.63
350	2.11	1.81	1.58	1.40	1.26	1.05	0.90	0.79	0.70	0.63
352	2.12	1.81	1.59	1.41	1.27	1.05	0.90	0.79	0.70	0.63
354	2.13	1.82	1.59	1.41	1.27	1.06	0.91	0.79	0.70	0.63
356	2.14	1.83	1.60	1.42	1.28	1.06	0.91	0.80	0.71	0.64
358	2.15	1.84	1.61	1.43	1.28	1.07	0.92	0.80	0.71	0.64
360	2.16	1.85	1.61	1.43	1.29	1.07	0.92	0.80	0.71	0.64
362	2.17	1.85	1.62	1.44	1.29	1.08	0.92	0.81	0.72	0.65
364	2.18	1.86	1.63	1.45	1.30	1.08	0.93	0.81	0.72	0.65
366	2.19	1.87	1.64	1.45	1.31	1.09	0.93	0.81	0.72	0.65
368	2.20	1.88	1.64	1.46	1.31	1.09	0.93	0.82	0.73	0.65
370	2.20	1.89	1.65	1.46	1.32	1.10	0.94	0.82	0.73	0.66
372	2.21	1.89	1.66	1.47	1.32	1.10	0.94	0.82	0.73	0.66
374	2.22	1.90	1.66	1.48	1.33	1.11	0.95	0.83	0.74	0.66
376	2.23	1.91	1.67	1.48	1.33	1.11	0.95	0.83	0.74	0.66
378	2.24	1.92	1.68	1.49	1.34	1.11	0.95	0.83	0.74	0.67
380	2.25	1.93	1.68	1.49	1.34	1.12	0.96	0.84	0.74	0.67
382	2.26	1.93	1.69	1.50	1.35	1.12	0.96	0.84	0.75	0.67
384	2.27	1.94	1.70	1.51	1.35	1.13	0.97	0.84	0.75	0.68
386	2.28	1.95	1.70	1.51	1.36	1.13	0.97	0.85	0.75	0.68
388	2.29	1.96	1.71	1.52	1.37	1.14	0.97	0.85	0.76	0.68
390	2.29	1.96	1.72	1.52	1.37	1.14	0.98	0.85	0.76	0.68
392	2.30	1.97	1.72	1.53	1.38	1.14	0.98	0.86	0.76	0.69
394	2.31	1.98	1.73	1.54	1.38	1.15	0.98	0.86	0.76	0.69
396	2.32	1.99	1.74	1.54	1.39	1.15	0.99	0.86	0.77	0.69
398	2.33	1.99	1.74	1.55	1.39	1.16	0.99	0.87	0.77	0.69
400	2.34	2.00	1.75	1.55	1.40	1.16	1.00	0.87	0.77	0.70

For notes on how to use the table see page 10

40

TABLE 1. RATES OF GROWTH (COMPOUNDING EACH PERIOD)

NUMBER OF PERIODS

FINAL AMOUNT	1	2	3	4	5	6	7	8	9	10
410			60.05	42.30	32.60	26.51	22.33	19.29	16.97	15.15
420			61.34	43.16	33.24	27.02	22.75	19.65	17.29	15.43
430			62.61	44.00	33.87	27.52	23.17	20.00	17.59	15.70
440			63.86	44.83	34.49	28.01	23.57	20.35	17.89	15.97
450			65.10	45.65	35.10	28.49	23.97	20.68	18.19	16.23
460			66.31	46.45	35.69	28.96	24.36	21.02	18.48	16.49
470			67.51	47.24	36.28	29.42	24.74	21.34	18.76	16.74
480			68.69	48.02	36.85	29.88	25.12	21.66	19.04	16.98
490			69.85	48.78	37.42	30.33	25.49	21.98	19.31	17.22
500			71.00	49.53	37.97	30.77	25.85	22.28	19.58	17.46
550			76.52	53.14	40.63	32.86	27.58	23.75	20.85	18.59
600			81.71	56.51	43.10	34.80	29.17	25.10	22.03	19.62
650			86.63	59.67	45.41	36.61	30.66	26.36	23.12	20.58
700			91.29	62.66	47.58	38.31	32.05	27.54	24.14	21.48
750			95.74	65.49	49.63	39.91	33.35	28.64	25.09	22.32
800				68.18	51.57	41.42	34.59	29.68	25.99	23.11
850				70.75	53.42	42.86	35.76	30.67	26.84	23.86
900				73.21	55.18	44.22	36.87	31.61	27.65	24.57
950				75.56	56.87	45.53	37.94	32.50	28.42	25.25
1000				77.83	58.49	46.78	38.95	33.35	29.15	25.89
1100				82.12	61.54	49.13	40.85	34.95	30.53	27.10
1200				86.12	64.38	51.31	42.62	36.43	31.80	28.21
1300				89.88	67.03	53.34	44.26	37.80	32.98	29.24
1400				93.43	69.52	55.25	45.79	39.08	34.07	30.20
1500				96.80	71.88	57.04	47.24	40.29	35.11	31.10
1600					74.11	58.74	48.60	41.42	36.08	31.95
1700					76.23	60.35	49.89	42.50	37.00	32.75
1800					78.26	61.89	51.12	43.52	37.87	33.51
1900					80.20	63.35	52.29	44.49	38.70	34.24
2000					82.06	64.75	53.41	45.42	39.50	34.93
2100					83.84	66.10	54.49	46.31	40.25	35.59
2200					85.56	67.39	55.52	47.16	40.98	36.22
2300					87.22	68.64	56.51	47.98	41.68	36.83
2400					88.82	69.84	57.46	48.77	42.35	37.41
2500					90.37	71.00	58.38	49.53	43.00	37.97
2600					91.86	72.12	59.27	50.27	43.62	38.52
2700					93.32	73.21	60.13	50.98	44.22	39.04
2800					94.73	74.26	60.97	51.67	44.81	39.55
2900					96.10	75.28	61.78	52.34	45.37	40.04
3000					97.44	76.27	62.56	52.98	45.92	40.51
3200						78.18	64.07	54.22	46.97	41.42
3400						79.99	65.49	55.39	47.97	42.28
3600						81.71	66.85	56.51	48.91	43.10
3800						83.36	68.14	57.57	49.81	43.87
4000						84.93	69.38	58.58	50.66	44.61
4200						86.44	70.57	59.55	51.48	45.32
4400						87.89	71.70	60.48	52.27	46.00
4600						89.29	72.80	61.38	53.02	46.65
4800						90.64	73.85	62.24	53.75	47.27
5000						91.94	74.87	63.07	54.45	47.88

For notes on how to use the table see page 10

TABLE 1. RATES OF GROWTH (COMPOUNDING EACH PERIOD)

NUMBER OF PERIODS

FINAL AMOUNT	11	12	13	14	15	16	17	18	19	20
410	13.69	12.48	11.46	10.60	9.86	9.22	8.65	8.15	7.71	7.31
420	13.94	12.70	11.67	10.79	10.04	9.38	8.81	8.30	7.85	7.44
430	14.18	12.92	11.87	10.98	10.21	9.54	8.96	8.44	7.98	7.57
440	14.42	13.14	12.07	11.16	10.38	9.70	9.11	8.58	8.11	7.69
450	14.65	13.35	12.27	11.34	10.55	9.86	9.25	8.72	8.24	7.81
460	14.88	13.56	12.46	11.52	10.71	10.01	9.39	8.85	8.36	7.93
470	15.11	13.76	12.64	11.69	10.87	10.16	9.53	8.98	8.49	8.05
480	15.33	13.96	12.82	11.86	11.02	10.30	9.67	9.11	8.61	8.16
490	15.54	14.16	13.00	12.02	11.18	10.44	9.80	9.23	8.72	8.27
500	15.76	14.35	13.18	12.18	11.33	10.58	9.93	9.35	8.84	8.38
550	16.76	15.26	14.01	12.95	12.04	11.24	10.55	9.93	9.39	8.90
600	17.69	16.10	14.78	13.65	12.69	11.85	11.12	10.47	9.89	9.37
650	18.55	16.88	15.49	14.31	13.29	12.41	11.64	10.96	10.35	9.81
700	19.35	17.60	16.15	14.91	13.85	12.93	12.13	11.42	10.78	10.22
750	20.10	18.28	16.76	15.48	14.38	13.42	12.58	11.84	11.19	10.60
800	20.81	18.92	17.35	16.01	14.87	13.88	13.01	12.25	11.57	10.96
850	21.48	19.52	17.89	16.52	15.34	14.31	13.42	12.62	11.92	11.29
900	22.11	20.09	18.41	16.99	15.78	14.72	13.80	12.98	12.26	11.61
950	22.71	20.64	18.91	17.45	16.19	15.11	14.16	13.32	12.58	11.91
1000	23.28	21.15	19.38	17.88	16.59	15.48	14.50	13.65	12.88	12.20
1100	24.36	22.12	20.26	18.68	17.33	16.17	15.15	14.25	13.45	12.74
1200	25.35	23.01	21.06	19.42	18.02	16.80	15.74	14.80	13.97	13.23
1300	26.26	23.83	21.81	20.11	18.65	17.39	16.29	15.31	14.45	13.68
1400	27.11	24.60	22.51	20.74	19.24	17.93	16.79	15.79	14.90	14.11
1500	27.91	25.32	23.16	21.34	19.79	18.44	17.27	16.24	15.32	14.50
1600	28.67	25.99	23.77	21.90	20.30	18.92	17.71	16.65	15.71	14.87
1700	29.38	26.63	24.35	22.43	20.79	19.37	18.14	17.05	16.08	15.22
1800	30.05	27.23	24.90	22.93	21.25	19.80	18.53	17.42	16.43	15.55
1900	30.69	27.81	25.42	23.41	21.69	20.20	18.91	17.77	16.76	15.86
2000	31.30	28.36	25.92	23.86	22.11	20.59	19.27	18.11	17.08	16.16
2100	31.89	28.88	26.39	24.29	22.50	20.96	19.61	18.43	17.38	16.44
2200	32.45	29.38	26.84	24.71	22.88	21.31	19.94	18.74	17.67	16.71
2300	32.98	29.86	27.28	25.10	23.25	21.65	20.25	19.03	17.94	16.97
2400	33.50	30.32	27.69	25.48	23.60	21.97	20.56	19.31	18.21	17.22
2500	33.99	30.77	28.10	25.85	23.94	22.28	20.85	19.58	18.46	17.46
2600	34.47	31.19	28.48	26.20	24.26	22.58	21.12	19.84	18.71	17.69
2700	34.93	31.61	28.86	26.54	24.57	22.87	21.39	20.09	18.94	17.91
2800	35.38	32.01	29.22	26.87	24.88	23.15	21.65	20.34	19.17	18.13
2900	35.81	32.39	29.57	27.19	25.17	23.42	21.91	20.57	19.39	18.34
3000	36.23	32.77	29.90	27.50	25.45	23.69	22.15	20.80	19.60	18.54
3200	37.04	33.48	30.55	28.09	25.99	24.19	22.61	21.23	20.01	18.92
3400	37.79	34.16	31.16	28.64	26.50	24.66	23.05	21.64	20.39	19.28
3600	38.51	34.80	31.74	29.17	26.99	25.10	23.47	22.03	20.76	19.62
3800	39.19	35.41	32.29	29.67	27.44	25.53	23.86	22.40	21.10	19.95
4000	39.84	35.99	32.81	30.15	27.88	25.93	24.23	22.74	21.43	20.25
4200	40.46	36.54	33.31	30.60	28.30	26.31	24.59	23.08	21.74	20.55
4400	41.06	37.07	33.79	31.04	28.70	26.68	24.93	23.40	22.04	20.83
4600	41.63	37.58	34.25	31.45	29.08	27.03	25.26	23.70	22.32	21.10
4800	42.18	38.07	34.69	31.85	29.44	27.37	25.57	23.99	22.60	21.36
5000	42.71	38.54	35.11	32.24	29.80	27.70	25.87	24.28	22 86	21.60

For notes on how to use the table see page 10

TABLE 1.   RATES OF GROWTH (COMPOUNDING EACH PERIOD)

NUMBER OF PERIODS

FINAL AMOUNT	21	22	23	24	25	26	27	28	29	30
410	6.95	6.62	6.33	6.06	5.81	5.58	5.36	5.17	4.99	4.82
420	7.07	6.74	6.44	6.16	5.91	5.67	5.46	5.26	5.07	4.90
430	7.19	6.85	6.55	6.27	6.01	5.77	5.55	5.35	5.16	4.98
440	7.31	6.97	6.65	6.37	6.11	5.86	5.64	5.43	5.24	5.06
450	7.42	7.08	6.76	6.47	6.20	5.96	5.73	5.52	5.32	5.14
460	7.54	7.18	6.86	6.57	6.29	6.05	5.81	5.60	5.40	5.22
470	7.65	7.29	6.96	6.66	6.39	6.13	5.90	5.68	5.48	5.29
480	7.76	7.39	7.06	6.75	6.48	6.22	5.98	5.76	5.56	5.37
490	7.86	7.49	7.15	6.85	6.56	6.30	6.06	5.84	5.63	5.44
500	7.97	7.59	7.25	6.94	6.65	6.39	6.14	5.92	5.71	5.51
550	8.46	8.06	7.69	7.36	7.06	6.78	6.52	6.28	6.05	5.85
600	8.91	8.49	8.10	7.75	7.43	7.13	6.86	6.61	6.37	6.15
650	9.32	8.88	8.48	8.11	7.77	7.46	7.18	6.91	6.67	6.44
700	9.71	9.25	8.83	8.45	8.09	7.77	7.47	7.20	6.94	6.70
750	10.07	9.59	9.16	8.76	8.39	8.06	7.75	7.46	7.19	6.95
800	10.41	9.91	9.46	9.05	8.67	8.33	8.01	7.71	7.43	7.18
850	10.73	10.22	9.75	9.33	8.94	8.58	8.25	7.94	7.66	7.39
900	11.03	10.50	10.02	9.59	9.19	8.82	8.48	8.16	7.87	7.60
950	11.32	10.78	10.28	9.83	9.42	9.04	8.70	8.37	8.07	7.79
1000	11.59	11.03	10.53	10.07	9.65	9.26	8.90	8.57	8.26	7.98
1100	12.10	11.52	10.99	10.51	10.07	9.66	9.29	8.94	8.62	8.32
1200	12.56	11.96	11.41	10.91	10.45	10.03	9.64	9.28	8.95	8.64
1300	12.99	12.37	11.80	11.28	10.80	10.37	9.97	9.59	9.25	8.93
1400	13.39	12.74	12.16	11.62	11.13	10.68	10.27	9.88	9.53	9.20
1500	13.76	13.10	12.50	11.94	11.44	10.98	10.55	10.15	9.79	9.45
1600	14.11	13.43	12.81	12.25	11.73	11.25	10.81	10.41	10.03	9.68
1700	14.44	13.74	13.11	12.53	12.00	11.51	11.06	10.65	10.26	9.90
1800	14.76	14.04	13.39	12.80	12.26	11.76	11.30	10.87	10.48	10.11
1900	15.05	14.32	13.66	13.05	12.50	11.99	11.52	11.09	10.69	10.31
2000	15.33	14.59	13.91	13.29	12.73	12.21	11.73	11.29	10.88	10.50
2100	15.60	14.84	14.15	13.53	12.95	12.42	11.94	11.49	11.07	10.68
2200	15.86	15.09	14.38	13.75	13.16	12.62	12.13	11.67	11.25	10.85
2300	16.10	15.32	14.61	13.96	13.36	12.82	12.31	11.85	11.42	11.02
2400	16.34	15.54	14.82	14.16	13.56	13.00	12.49	12.02	11.58	11.17
2500	16.57	15.76	15.02	14.35	13.74	13.18	12.66	12.18	11.74	11.33
2600	16.78	15.96	15.22	14.54	13.92	13.35	12.83	12.34	11.89	11.47
2700	16.99	16.16	15.41	14.72	14.09	13.51	12.98	12.49	12.04	11.61
2800	17.20	16.35	15.59	14.89	14.26	13.67	13.14	12.64	12.18	11.75
2900	17.39	16.54	15.77	15.06	14.42	13.83	13.28	12.78	12.31	11.88
3000	17.58	16.72	15.94	15.23	14.57	13.98	13.42	12.92	12.44	12.00
3200	17.94	17.06	16.26	15.54	14.87	14.26	13.70	13.18	12.69	12.25
3400	18.28	17.39	16.57	15.83	15.15	14.53	13.95	13.42	12.93	12.47
3600	18.61	17.69	16.86	16.10	15.41	14.78	14.19	13.65	13.15	12.69
3800	18.91	17.98	17.13	16.37	15.66	15.02	14.42	13.87	13.36	12.89
4000	19.20	18.26	17.40	16.61	15.90	15.24	14.64	14.08	13.56	13.08
4200	19.48	18.52	17.65	16.85	16.13	15.46	14.85	14.28	13.76	13.27
4400	19.75	18.77	17.88	17.08	16.34	15.67	15.05	14.47	13.94	13.44
4600	20.00	19.01	18.11	17.30	16.55	15.86	15.23	14.65	14.11	13.61
4800	20.24	19.24	18.33	17.50	16.75	16.05	15.42	14.83	14.28	13.77
5000	20.48	19.46	18.54	17.70	16.94	16.24	15.59	14.99	14.44	13.93

For notes on how to use the table see page 10

TABLE 1. RATES OF GROWTH (COMPOUNDING EACH PERIOD)

NUMBER OF PERIODS

FINAL AMOUNT	31	32	33	34	35	36	37	38	39	40
410	4.66	4.51	4.37	4.24	4.11	4.00	3.89	3.78	3.68	3.59
420	4.74	4.59	4.44	4.31	4.19	4.07	3.95	3.85	3.75	3.65
430	4.82	4.66	4.52	4.38	4.26	4.13	4.02	3.91	3.81	3.71
440	4.90	4.74	4.59	4.45	4.32	4.20	4.09	3.98	3.87	3.77
450	4.97	4.81	4.66	4.52	4.39	4.27	4.15	4.04	3.93	3.83
460	5.05	4.88	4.73	4.59	4.46	4.33	4.21	4.10	3.99	3.89
470	5.12	4.95	4.80	4.66	4.52	4.39	4.27	4.16	4.05	3.94
480	5.19	5.02	4.87	4.72	4.58	4.45	4.33	4.21	4.10	4.00
490	5.26	5.09	4.93	4.79	4.65	4.51	4.39	4.27	4.16	4.05
500	5.33	5.16	5.00	4.85	4.71	4.57	4.45	4.33	4.21	4.11
550	5.65	5.47	5.30	5.14	4.99	4.85	4.72	4.59	4.47	4.35
600	5.95	5.76	5.58	5.41	5.25	5.10	4.96	4.83	4.70	4.58
650	6.22	6.02	5.84	5.66	5.49	5.34	5.19	5.05	4.92	4.79
700	6.48	6.27	6.07	5.89	5.72	5.55	5.40	5.25	5.12	4.99
750	6.72	6.50	6.30	6.11	5.93	5.76	5.60	5.45	5.30	5.17
800	6.94	6.71	6.50	6.31	6.12	5.95	5.78	5.62	5.48	5.34
850	7.15	6.92	6.70	6.50	6.31	6.12	5.95	5.79	5.64	5.50
900	7.35	7.11	6.88	6.68	6.48	6.29	6.12	5.95	5.80	5.65
950	7.53	7.29	7.06	6.85	6.64	6.45	6.27	6.10	5.94	5.79
1000	7.71	7.46	7.23	7.01	6.80	6.61	6.42	6.25	6.08	5.93
1100	8.04	7.78	7.54	7.31	7.09	6.89	6.70	6.51	6.34	6.18
1200	8.35	8.07	7.82	7.58	7.36	7.15	6.95	6.76	6.58	6.41
1300	8.63	8.35	8.08	7.84	7.60	7.38	7.18	6.98	6.80	6.62
1400	8.89	8.60	8.33	8.07	7.83	7.61	7.39	7.19	7.00	6.82
1500	9.13	8.83	8.55	8.29	8.04	7.81	7.59	7.39	7.19	7.00
1600	9.36	9.05	8.76	8.50	8.24	8.01	7.78	7.57	7.37	7.18
1700	9.57	9.26	8.96	8.69	8.43	8.19	7.96	7.74	7.54	7.34
1800	9.77	9.45	9.15	8.87	8.61	8.36	8.13	7.90	7.69	7.49
1900	9.96	9.64	9.33	9.05	8.78	8.52	8.28	8.06	7.84	7.64
2000	10.15	9.81	9.50	9.21	8.94	8.68	8.43	8.20	7.98	7.78
2100	10.32	9.98	9.66	9.37	9.09	8.82	8.58	8.34	8.12	7.91
2200	10.49	10.14	9.82	9.52	9.23	8.97	8.71	8.47	8.25	8.03
2300	10.64	10.29	9.97	9.66	9.37	9.10	8.84	8.60	8.37	8.15
2400	10.80	10.44	10.11	9.80	9.51	9.23	8.97	8.72	8.49	8.27
2500	10.94	10.58	10.25	9.93	9.63	9.35	9.09	8.84	8.60	8.38
2600	11.08	10.72	10.38	10.06	9.76	9.47	9.20	8.95	8.71	8.49
2700	11.22	10.85	10.50	10.18	9.87	9.59	9.32	9.06	8.82	8.59
2800	11.35	10.97	10.62	10.30	9.99	9.70	9.42	9.16	8.92	8.69
2900	11.47	11.10	10.74	10.41	10.10	9.81	9.53	9.27	9.02	8.78
3000	11.60	11.21	10.86	10.52	10.21	9.91	9.63	9.36	9.11	8.87
3200	11.83	11.44	11.07	10.73	10.41	10.11	9.82	9.55	9.29	9.05
3400	12.05	11.65	11.28	10.93	10.60	10.29	10.00	9.72	9.46	9.22
3600	12.25	11.85	11.47	11.12	10.78	10.47	10.17	9.89	9.62	9.37
3800	12.45	12.04	11.65	11.29	10.95	10.63	10.33	10.05	9.78	9.52
4000	12.64	12.22	11.83	11.46	11.12	10.79	10.48	10.19	9.92	9.66
4200	12.81	12.39	11.99	11.62	11.27	10.94	10.63	10.34	10.06	9.79
4400	12.98	12.55	12.15	11.77	11.42	11.08	10.77	10.47	10.19	9.92
4600	13.15	12.71	12.30	11.92	11.56	11.22	10.90	10.60	10.32	10.04
4800	13.30	12.86	12.45	12.06	11.70	11.35	11.03	10.72	10.44	10.16
5000	13.45	13.00	12.59	12.19	11.83	11.48	11.15	10.84	10.55	10.27

For notes on how to use the table see page 10

TABLE 1. RATES OF GROWTH (COMPOUNDING EACH PERIOD)

NUMBER OF PERIODS

FINAL AMOUNT	41	42	43	44	45	46	47	48	49	50
410	3.50	3.42	3.34	3.26	3.19	3.11	3.05	2.98	2.92	2.86
420	3.56	3.48	3.39	3.32	3.24	3.17	3.10	3.03	2.97	2.91
430	3.62	3.53	3.45	3.37	3.29	3.22	3.15	3.09	3.02	2.96
440	3.68	3.59	3.51	3.42	3.35	3.27	3.20	3.13	3.07	3.01
450	3.74	3.65	3.56	3.48	3.40	3.32	3.25	3.18	3.12	3.05
460	3.79	3.70	3.61	3.53	3.45	3.37	3.30	3.23	3.16	3.10
470	3.85	3.75	3.66	3.58	3.50	3.42	3.35	3.28	3.21	3.14
480	3.90	3.81	3.72	3.63	3.55	3.47	3.39	3.32	3.25	3.19
490	3.95	3.86	3.77	3.68	3.59	3.52	3.44	3.37	3.30	3.23
500	4.00	3.91	3.81	3.73	3.64	3.56	3.48	3.41	3.34	3.27
550	4.25	4.14	4.04	3.95	3.86	3.78	3.69	3.62	3.54	3.47
600	4.47	4.36	4.25	4.16	4.06	3.97	3.89	3.80	3.72	3.65
650	4.67	4.56	4.45	4.35	4.25	4.15	4.06	3.98	3.89	3.81
700	4.86	4.74	4.63	4.52	4.42	4.32	4.23	4.14	4.05	3.97
750	5.04	4.91	4.80	4.69	4.58	4.48	4.38	4.29	4.20	4.11
800	5.20	5.08	4.95	4.84	4.73	4.62	4.52	4.43	4.34	4.25
850	5.36	5.23	5.10	4.98	4.87	4.76	4.66	4.56	4.46	4.37
900	5.51	5.37	5.24	5.12	5.00	4.89	4.79	4.68	4.59	4.49
950	5.64	5.51	5.38	5.25	5.13	5.02	4.91	4.80	4.70	4.61
1000	5.78	5.64	5.50	5.37	5.25	5.13	5.02	4.91	4.81	4.71
1100	6.02	5.88	5.73	5.60	5.47	5.35	5.23	5.12	5.02	4.91
1200	6.25	6.09	5.95	5.81	5.68	5.55	5.43	5.31	5.20	5.10
1300	6.46	6.30	6.15	6.00	5.87	5.73	5.61	5.49	5.37	5.26
1400	6.65	6.49	6.33	6.18	6.04	5.90	5.78	5.65	5.53	5.42
1500	6.83	6.66	6.50	6.35	6.20	6.06	5.93	5.80	5.68	5.57
1600	7.00	6.82	6.66	6.50	6.36	6.21	6.08	5.95	5.82	5.70
1700	7.15	6.98	6.81	6.65	6.50	6.35	6.21	6.08	5.95	5.83
1800	7.30	7.12	6.95	6.79	6.63	6.49	6.34	6.21	6.08	5.95
1900	7.45	7.26	7.09	6.92	6.76	6.61	6.47	6.33	6.19	6.07
2000	7.58	7.39	7.22	7.05	6.88	6.73	6.58	6.44	6.30	6.17
2100	7.71	7.52	7.34	7.16	7.00	6.84	6.69	6.55	6.41	6.28
2200	7.83	7.64	7.45	7.28	7.11	6.95	6.80	6.65	6.51	6.38
2300	7.95	7.75	7.56	7.39	7.22	7.05	6.90	6.75	6.61	6.47
2400	8.06	7.86	7.67	7.49	7.32	7.15	7.00	6.85	6.70	6.56
2500	8.17	7.97	7.77	7.59	7.42	7.25	7.09	6.94	6.79	6.65
2600	8.27	8.07	7.87	7.69	7.51	7.34	7.18	7.02	6.88	6.73
2700	8.37	8.16	7.97	7.78	7.60	7.43	7.26	7.11	6.96	6.81
2800	8.47	8.26	8.06	7.87	7.69	7.51	7.35	7.19	7.04	6.89
2900	8.56	8.35	8.15	7.95	7.77	7.59	7.43	7.27	7.11	6.97
3000	8.65	8.44	8.23	8.04	7.85	7.67	7.50	7.34	7.19	7.04
3200	8.82	8.60	8.39	8.20	8.01	7.83	7.65	7.49	7.33	7.18
3400	8.98	8.76	8.55	8.34	8.15	7.97	7.79	7.62	7.46	7.31
3600	9.13	8.91	8.69	8.49	8.29	8.10	7.92	7.75	7.59	7.43
3800	9.28	9.05	8.83	8.62	8.42	8.23	8.05	7.87	7.71	7.55
4000	9.41	9.18	8.96	8.75	8.54	8.35	8.16	7.99	7.82	7.66
4200	9.54	9.31	9.08	8.87	8.66	8.46	8.28	8.10	7.93	7.76
4400	9.67	9.43	9.20	8.98	8.77	8.57	8.38	8.20	8.03	7.86
4600	9.79	9.54	9.31	9.09	8.88	8.68	8.49	8.30	8.13	7.96
4800	9.90	9.66	9.42	9.20	8.98	8.78	8.59	8.40	8.22	8.05
5000	10.01	9.76	9.52	9.30	9.08	8.88	8.68	8.49	8.31	8.14

For notes on how to use the table see page 10

TABLE 1. RATES OF GROWTH (COMPOUNDING EACH PERIOD)

NUMBER OF PERIODS

FINAL AMOUNT	60	70	80	90	100	120	140	160	180	200
410	2.38	2.04	1.78	1.58	1.42	1.18	1.01	0.89	0.79	0.71
420	2.42	2.07	1.81	1.61	1.45	1.20	1.03	0.90	0.80	0.72
430	2.46	2.11	1.84	1.63	1.47	1.22	1.05	0.92	0.81	0.73
440	2.50	2.14	1.87	1.66	1.49	1.24	1.06	0.93	0.83	0.74
450	2.54	2.17	1.90	1.69	1.52	1.26	1.08	0.94	0.84	0.75
460	2.58	2.20	1.93	1.71	1.54	1.28	1.10	0.96	0.85	0.77
470	2.61	2.24	1.95	1.73	1.56	1.30	1.11	0.97	0.86	0.78
480	2.65	2.27	1.98	1.76	1.58	1.32	1.13	0.99	0.88	0.79
490	2.68	2.30	2.01	1.78	1.60	1.33	1.14	1.00	0.89	0.80
500	2.72	2.33	2.03	1.80	1.62	1.35	1.16	1.01	0.90	0.81
550	2.88	2.47	2.15	1.91	1.72	1.43	1.23	1.07	0.95	0.86
600	3.03	2.59	2.26	2.01	1.81	1.50	1.29	1.13	1.00	0.90
650	3.17	2.71	2.37	2.10	1.89	1.57	1.35	1.18	1.05	0.94
700	3.30	2.82	2.46	2.19	1.96	1.63	1.40	1.22	1.09	0.98
750	3.42	2.92	2.55	2.26	2.04	1.69	1.45	1.27	1.13	1.01
800	3.53	3.02	2.63	2.34	2.10	1.75	1.50	1.31	1.16	1.05
850	3.63	3.10	2.71	2.41	2.16	1.80	1.54	1.35	1.20	1.08
900	3.73	3.19	2.78	2.47	2.22	1.85	1.58	1.38	1.23	1.10
950	3.82	3.27	2.85	2.53	2.28	1.89	1.62	1.42	1.26	1.13
1000	3.91	3.34	2.92	2.59	2.33	1.94	1.66	1.45	1.29	1.16
1100	4.08	3.48	3.04	2.70	2.43	2.02	1.73	1.51	1.34	1.21
1200	4.23	3.61	3.15	2.80	2.52	2.09	1.79	1.57	1.39	1.25
1300	4.37	3.73	3.26	2.89	2.60	2.16	1.85	1.62	1.44	1.29
1400	4.50	3.84	3.35	2.98	2.67	2.22	1.90	1.66	1.48	1.33
1500	4.62	3.94	3.44	3.05	2.75	2.28	1.95	1.71	1.52	1.36
1600	4.73	4.04	3.53	3.13	2.81	2.34	2.00	1.75	1.55	1.40
1700	4.84	4.13	3.60	3.20	2.87	2.39	2.04	1.79	1.59	1.43
1800	4.94	4.22	3.68	3.26	2.93	2.44	2.09	1.82	1.62	1.46
1900	5.03	4.30	3.75	3.33	2.99	2.48	2.13	1.86	1.65	1.48
2000	5.12	4.37	3.82	3.38	3.04	2.53	2.16	1.89	1.68	1.51
2100	5.21	4.45	3.88	3.44	3.09	2.57	2.20	1.92	1.71	1.53
2200	5.29	4.51	3.94	3.49	3.14	2.61	2.23	1.95	1.73	1.56
2300	5.36	4.58	4.00	3.55	3.19	2.65	2.26	1.98	1.76	1.58
2400	5.44	4.64	4.05	3.59	3.23	2.68	2.30	2.01	1.78	1.60
2500	5.51	4.71	4.11	3.64	3.27	2.72	2.33	2.03	1.80	1.62
2600	5.58	4.76	4.16	3.69	3.31	2.75	2.35	2.06	1.83	1.64
2700	5.65	4.82	4.21	3.73	3.35	2.78	2.38	2.08	1.85	1.66
2800	5.71	4.88	4.25	3.77	3.39	2.82	2.41	2.10	1.87	1.68
2900	5.77	4.93	4.30	3.81	3.42	2.85	2.43	2.13	1.89	1.70
3000	5.83	4.98	4.34	3.85	3.46	2.87	2.46	2.15	1.91	1.72
3200	5.95	5.08	4.43	3.93	3.53	2.93	2.51	2.19	1.94	1.75
3400	6.05	5.17	4.51	4.00	3.59	2.98	2.55	2.23	1.98	1.78
3600	6.15	5.25	4.58	4.06	3.65	3.03	2.59	2.26	2.01	1.81
3800	6.25	5.33	4.65	4.12	3.70	3.08	2.63	2.30	2.04	1.84
4000	6.34	5.41	4.72	4.18	3.76	3.12	2.67	2.33	2.07	1.86
4200	6.43	5.48	4.78	4.24	3.81	3.16	2.71	2.36	2.10	1.89
4400	6.51	5.55	4.84	4.29	3.86	3.20	2.74	2.39	2.12	1.91
4600	6.59	5.62	4.90	4.35	3.90	3.24	2.77	2.42	2.15	1.93
4800	6.66	5.69	4.96	4.40	3.95	3.28	2.80	2.45	2.17	1.95
5000	6.74	5.75	5.01	4.44	3.99	3.31	2.83	2.48	2.20	1.98

For notes on how to use the table see page 10

Table 2

RATES OF GROWTH

(Compounding Continuously)

TABLE 2.   RATES OF GROWTH   (COMPOUNDING CONTINUOUSLY)

NUMBER OF PERIODS

FINAL AMOUNT	1	2	3	4	5	6	7	8	9	10
101	1.00	0.50	0.33	0.25	0.20	0.17	0.14	0.12	0.11	0.10
102	1.98	0.99	0.66	0.50	0.40	0.33	0.28	0.25	0.22	0.20
103	2.96	1.48	0.99	0.74	0.59	0.49	0.42	0.37	0.33	0.30
104	3.92	1.96	1.31	0.98	0.78	0.65	0.56	0.49	0.44	0.39
105	4.88	2.44	1.63	1.22	0.98	0.81	0.70	0.61	0.54	0.49
106	5.83	2.91	1.94	1.46	1.17	0.97	0.83	0.73	0.65	0.58
107	6.77	3.38	2.26	1.69	1.35	1.13	0.97	0.85	0.75	0.68
108	7.70	3.85	2.57	1.92	1.54	1.28	1.10	0.96	0.86	0.77
109	8.62	4.31	2.87	2.15	1.72	1.44	1.23	1.08	0.96	0.86
110	9.53	4.77	3.18	2.38	1.91	1.59	1.36	1.19	1.06	0.95
111	10.44	5.22	3.48	2.61	2.09	1.74	1.49	1.30	1.16	1.04
112	11.33	5.67	3.78	2.83	2.27	1.89	1.62	1.42	1.26	1.13
113	12.22	6.11	4.07	3.06	2.44	2.04	1.75	1.53	1.36	1.22
114	13.10	6.55	4.37	3.28	2.62	2.18	1.87	1.64	1.46	1.31
115	13.98	6.99	4.66	3.49	2.80	2.33	2.00	1.75	1.55	1.40
116	14.84	7.42	4.95	3.71	2.97	2.47	2.12	1.86	1.65	1.48
117	15.70	7.85	5.23	3.93	3.14	2.62	2.24	1.96	1.74	1.57
118	16.55	8.28	5.52	4.14	3.31	2.76	2.36	2.07	1.84	1.66
119	17.40	8.70	5.80	4.35	3.48	2.90	2.49	2.17	1.93	1.74
120	18.23	9.12	6.08	4.56	3.65	3.04	2.60	2.28	2.03	1.82
121	19.06	9.53	6.35	4.77	3.81	3.18	2.72	2.38	2.12	1.91
122	19.89	9.94	6.63	4.97	3.98	3.31	2.84	2.49	2.21	1.99
123	20.70	10.35	6.90	5.18	4.14	3.45	2.96	2.59	2.30	2.07
124	21.51	10.76	7.17	5.38	4.30	3.59	3.07	2.69	2.39	2.15
125	22.31	11.16	7.44	5.58	4.46	3.72	3.19	2.79	2.48	2.23
126	23.11	11.56	7.70	5.78	4.62	3.85	3.30	2.89	2.57	2.31
127	23.90	11.95	7.97	5.98	4.78	3.98	3.41	2.99	2.66	2.39
128	24.69	12.34	8.23	6.17	4.94	4.11	3.53	3.09	2.74	2.47
129	25.46	12.73	8.49	6.37	5.09	4.24	3.64	3.18	2.83	2.55
130	26.24	13.12	8.75	6.56	5.25	4.37	3.75	3.28	2.92	2.62
131	27.00	13.50	9.00	6.75	5.40	4.50	3.86	3.38	3.00	2.70
132	27.76	13.88	9.25	6.94	5.55	4.63	3.97	3.47	3.08	2.78
133	28.52	14.26	9.51	7.13	5.70	4.75	4.07	3.56	3.17	2.85
134	29.27	14.63	9.76	7.32	5.85	4.88	4.18	3.66	3.25	2.93
135	30.01	15.01	10.00	7.50	6.00	5.00	4.29	3.75	3.33	3.00
136	30.75	15.37	10.25	7.69	6.15	5.12	4.39	3.84	3.42	3.07
137	31.48	15.74	10.49	7.87	6.30	5.25	4.50	3.94	3.50	3.15
138	32.21	16.10	10.74	8.05	6.44	5.37	4.60	4.03	3.58	3.22
139	32.93	16.47	10.98	8.23	6.59	5.49	4.70	4.12	3.66	3.29
140	33.65	16.82	11.22	8.41	6.73	5.61	4.81	4.21	3.74	3.36
141	34.36	17.18	11.45	8.59	6.87	5.73	4.91	4.29	3.82	3.44
142	35.07	17.53	11.69	8.77	7.01	5.84	5.01	4.38	3.90	3.51
143	35.77	17.88	11.92	8.94	7.15	5.96	5.11	4.47	3.97	3.58
144	36.46	18.23	12.15	9.12	7.29	6.08	5.21	4.56	4.05	3.65
145	37.16	18.58	12.39	9.29	7.43	6.19	5.31	4.64	4.13	3.72
146	37.84	18.92	12.61	9.46	7.57	6.31	5.41	4.73	4.20	3.78
147	38.53	19.26	12.84	9.63	7.71	6.42	5.50	4.82	4.28	3.85
148	39.20	19.60	13.07	9.80	7.84	6.53	5.60	4.90	4.36	3.92
149	39.88	19.94	13.29	9.97	7.98	6.65	5.70	4.98	4.43	3.99
150	40.55	20.27	13.52	10.14	8.11	6.76	5.79	5.07	4.51	4.05

For notes on how to use the table see page 12

TABLE 2.   RATES OF GROWTH   (COMPOUNDING CONTINUOUSLY)

NUMBER OF PERIODS

FINAL AMOUNT	12	14	16	18	20	22	24	26	28	30
101	0.08	0.07	0.06	0.06	0.05	0.05	0.04	0.04	0.04	0.03
102	0.17	0.14	0.12	0.11	0.10	0.09	0.08	0.08	0.07	0.07
103	0.25	0.21	0.18	0.16	0.15	0.13	0.12	0.11	0.11	0.10
104	0.33	0.28	0.25	0.22	0.20	0.18	0.16	0.15	0.14	0.13
105	0.41	0.35	0.30	0.27	0.24	0.22	0.20	0.19	0.17	0.16
106	0.49	0.42	0.36	0.32	0.29	0.26	0.24	0.22	0.21	0.19
107	0.56	0.48	0.42	0.38	0.34	0.31	0.28	0.26	0.24	0.23
108	0.64	0.55	0.48	0.43	0.38	0.35	0.32	0.30	0.27	0.26
109	0.72	0.62	0.54	0.48	0.43	0.39	0.36	0.33	0.31	0.29
110	0.79	0.68	0.60	0.53	0.48	0.43	0.40	0.37	0.34	0.32
111	0.87	0.75	0.65	0.58	0.52	0.47	0.43	0.40	0.37	0.35
112	0.94	0.81	0.71	0.63	0.57	0.52	0.47	0.44	0.40	0.38
113	1.02	0.87	0.76	0.68	0.61	0.56	0.51	0.47	0.44	0.41
114	1.09	0.94	0.82	0.73	0.66	0.60	0.55	0.50	0.47	0.44
115	1.16	1.00	0.87	0.78	0.70	0.64	0.58	0.54	0.50	0.47
116	1.24	1.06	0.93	0.82	0.74	0.67	0.62	0.57	0.53	0.49
117	1.31	1.12	0.98	0.87	0.79	0.71	0.65	0.60	0.56	0.52
118	1.38	1.18	1.03	0.92	0.83	0.75	0.69	0.64	0.59	0.55
119	1.45	1.24	1.09	0.97	0.87	0.79	0.72	0.67	0.62	0.58
120	1.52	1.30	1.14	1.01	0.91	0.83	0.76	0.70	0.65	0.61
121	1.59	1.36	1.19	1.06	0.95	0.87	0.79	0.73	0.68	0.64
122	1.66	1.42	1.24	1.10	0.99	0.90	0.83	0.76	0.71	0.66
123	1.73	1.48	1.29	1.15	1.04	0.94	0.86	0.80	0.74	0.69
124	1.79	1.54	1.34	1.20	1.08	0.98	0.90	0.83	0.77	0.72
125	1.86	1.59	1.39	1.24	1.12	1.01	0.93	0.86	0.80	0.74
126	1.93	1.65	1.44	1.28	1.16	1.05	0.96	0.89	0.83	0.77
127	1.99	1.71	1.49	1.33	1.20	1.09	1.00	0.92	0.85	0.80
128	2.06	1.76	1.54	1.37	1.23	1.12	1.03	0.95	0.88	0.82
129	2.12	1.82	1.59	1.41	1.27	1.16	1.06	0.98	0.91	0.85
130	2.19	1.87	1.64	1.46	1.31	1.19	1.09	1.01	0.94	0.87
131	2.25	1.93	1.69	1.50	1.35	1.23	1.13	1.04	0.96	0.90
132	2.31	1.98	1.74	1.54	1.39	1.26	1.16	1.07	0.99	0.93
133	2.38	2.04	1.78	1.58	1.43	1.30	1.19	1.10	1.02	0.95
134	2.44	2.09	1.83	1.63	1.46	1.33	1.22	1.13	1.05	0.98
135	2.50	2.14	1.88	1.67	1.50	1.36	1.25	1.15	1.07	1.00
136	2.56	2.20	1.92	1.71	1.54	1.40	1.28	1.18	1.10	1.02
137	2.62	2.25	1.97	1.75	1.57	1.43	1.31	1.21	1.12	1.05
138	2.68	2.30	2.01	1.79	1.61	1.46	1.34	1.24	1.15	1.07
139	2.74	2.35	2.06	1.83	1.65	1.50	1.37	1.27	1.18	1.10
140	2.80	2.40	2.10	1.87	1.68	1.53	1.40	1.29	1.20	1.12
141	2.86	2.45	2.15	1.91	1.72	1.56	1.43	1.32	1.23	1.15
142	2.92	2.50	2.19	1.95	1.75	1.59	1.46	1.35	1.25	1.17
143	2.98	2.55	2.24	1.99	1.79	1.63	1.49	1.38	1.28	1.19
144	3.04	2.60	2.28	2.03	1.82	1.66	1.52	1.40	1.30	1.22
145	3.10	2.65	2.32	2.06	1.86	1.69	1.55	1.43	1.33	1.24
146	3.15	2.70	2.37	2.10	1.89	1.72	1.58	1.46	1.35	1.26
147	3.21	2.75	2.41	2.14	1.93	1.75	1.61	1.48	1.38	1.28
148	3.27	2.80	2.45	2.18	1.96	1.78	1.63	1.51	1.40	1.31
149	3.32	2.85	2.49	2.22	1.99	1.81	1.66	1.53	1.42	1.33
150	3.38	2.90	2.53	2.25	2.03	1.84	1.69	1.56	1.45	1.35

For notes on how to use the table see page 12

TABLE 2. RATES OF GROWTH (COMPOUNDING CONTINUOUSLY)

NUMBER OF PERIODS

FINAL AMOUNT	32	34	36	38	40	42	44	46	48	50
101	0.03	0.03	0.03	0.03	0.02	0.02	0.02	0.02	0.02	0.02
102	0.06	0.06	0.06	0.05	0.05	0.05	0.05	0.04	0.04	0.04
103	0.09	0.09	0.08	0.08	0.07	0.07	0.07	0.06	0.06	0.06
104	0.12	0.12	0.11	0.10	0.10	0.09	0.09	0.09	0.08	0.08
105	0.15	0.14	0.14	0.13	0.12	0.12	0.11	0.11	0.10	0.10
106	0.18	0.17	0.16	0.15	0.15	0.14	0.13	0.13	0.12	0.12
107	0.21	0.20	0.19	0.18	0.17	0.16	0.15	0.15	0.14	0.14
108	0.24	0.23	0.21	0.20	0.19	0.18	0.17	0.17	0.16	0.15
109	0.27	0.25	0.24	0.23	0.22	0.21	0.20	0.19	0.18	0.17
110	0.30	0.28	0.26	0.25	0.24	0.23	0.22	0.21	0.20	0.19
111	0.33	0.31	0.29	0.27	0.26	0.25	0.24	0.23	0.22	0.21
112	0.35	0.33	0.31	0.30	0.28	0.27	0.26	0.25	0.24	0.23
113	0.38	0.36	0.34	0.32	0.31	0.29	0.28	0.27	0.25	0.24
114	0.41	0.39	0.36	0.34	0.33	0.31	0.30	0.28	0.27	0.26
115	0.44	0.41	0.39	0.37	0.35	0.33	0.32	0.30	0.29	0.28
116	0.46	0.44	0.41	0.39	0.37	0.35	0.34	0.32	0.31	0.30
117	0.49	0.46	0.44	0.41	0.39	0.37	0.36	0.34	0.33	0.31
118	0.52	0.49	0.46	0.44	0.41	0.39	0.38	0.36	0.34	0.33
119	0.54	0.51	0.48	0.46	0.43	0.41	0.40	0.38	0.36	0.35
120	0.57	0.54	0.51	0.48	0.46	0.43	0.41	0.40	0.38	0.36
121	0.60	0.56	0.53	0.50	0.48	0.45	0.43	0.41	0.40	0.38
122	0.62	0.58	0.55	0.52	0.50	0.47	0.45	0.43	0.41	0.40
123	0.65	0.61	0.58	0.54	0.52	0.49	0.47	0.45	0.43	0.41
124	0.67	0.63	0.60	0.57	0.54	0.51	0.49	0.47	0.45	0.43
125	0.70	0.66	0.62	0.59	0.56	0.53	0.51	0.49	0.46	0.45
126	0.72	0.68	0.64	0.61	0.58	0.55	0.53	0.50	0.48	0.46
127	0.75	0.70	0.66	0.63	0.60	0.57	0.54	0.52	0.50	0.48
128	0.77	0.73	0.69	0.65	0.62	0.59	0.56	0.54	0.51	0.49
129	0.80	0.75	0.71	0.67	0.64	0.61	0.58	0.55	0.53	0.51
130	0.82	0.77	0.73	0.69	0.66	0.62	0.60	0.57	0.55	0.52
131	0.84	0.79	0.75	0.71	0.68	0.64	0.61	0.59	0.56	0.54
132	0.87	0.82	0.77	0.73	0.69	0.66	0.63	0.60	0.58	0.56
133	0.89	0.84	0.79	0.75	0.71	0.68	0.65	0.62	0.59	0.57
134	0.91	0.86	0.81	0.77	0.73	0.70	0.67	0.64	0.61	0.59
135	0.94	0.88	0.83	0.79	0.75	0.71	0.68	0.65	0.63	0.60
136	0.96	0.90	0.85	0.81	0.77	0.73	0.70	0.67	0.64	0.61
137	0.98	0.93	0.87	0.83	0.79	0.75	0.72	0.68	0.66	0.63
138	1.01	0.95	0.89	0.85	0.81	0.77	0.73	0.70	0.67	0.64
139	1.03	0.97	0.91	0.87	0.82	0.78	0.75	0.72	0.69	0.66
140	1.05	0.99	0.93	0.89	0.84	0.80	0.76	0.73	0.70	0.67
141	1.07	1.01	0.95	0.90	0.86	0.82	0.78	0.75	0.72	0.69
142	1.10	1.03	0.97	0.92	0.88	0.83	0.80	0.76	0.73	0.70
143	1.12	1.05	0.99	0.94	0.89	0.85	0.81	0.78	0.75	0.72
144	1.14	1.07	1.01	0.96	0.91	0.87	0.83	0.79	0.76	0.73
145	1.16	1.09	1.03	0.98	0.93	0.88	0.84	0.81	0.77	0.74
146	1.18	1.11	1.05	1.00	0.95	0.90	0.86	0.82	0.79	0.76
147	1.20	1.13	1.07	1.01	0.96	0.92	0.88	0.84	0.80	0.77
148	1.23	1.15	1.09	1.03	0.98	0.93	0.89	0.85	0.82	0.78
149	1.25	1.17	1.11	1.05	1.00	0.95	0.91	0.87	0.83	0.80
150	1.27	1.19	1.13	1.07	1.01	0.97	0.92	0.88	0.84	0.81

For notes on how to use the table see page 12

TABLE 2. RATES OF GROWTH (COMPOUNDING CONTINUOUSLY)

NUMBER OF PERIODS

FINAL AMOUNT	60	70	80	90	100	120	140	160	180	200
101	0.02	0.01	0.01	0.01	0.01	0.01	0.01	0.01	0.01	0.00
102	0.03	0.03	0.02	0.02	0.02	0.02	0.01	0.01	0.01	0.01
103	0.05	0.04	0.04	0.03	0.03	0.02	0.02	0.02	0.02	0.01
104	0.07	0.06	0.05	0.04	0.04	0.03	0.03	0.02	0.02	0.02
105	0.08	0.07	0.06	0.05	0.05	0.04	0.03	0.03	0.03	0.02
106	0.10	0.08	0.07	0.06	0.06	0.05	0.04	0.04	0.03	0.03
107	0.11	0.10	0.08	0.08	0.07	0.06	0.05	0.04	0.04	0.03
108	0.13	0.11	0.10	0.09	0.08	0.06	0.05	0.05	0.04	0.04
109	0.14	0.12	0.11	0.10	0.09	0.07	0.06	0.05	0.05	0.04
110	0.16	0.14	0.12	0.11	0.10	0.08	0.07	0.06	0.05	0.05
111	0.17	0.15	0.13	0.12	0.10	0.09	0.07	0.07	0.06	0.05
112	0.19	0.16	0.14	0.13	0.11	0.09	0.08	0.07	0.06	0.06
113	0.20	0.17	0.15	0.14	0.12	0.10	0.09	0.08	0.07	0.06
114	0.22	0.19	0.16	0.15	0.13	0.11	0.09	0.08	0.07	0.07
115	0.23	0.20	0.17	0.16	0.14	0.12	0.10	0.09	0.08	0.07
116	0.25	0.21	0.19	0.16	0.15	0.12	0.11	0.09	0.08	0.07
117	0.26	0.22	0.20	0.17	0.16	0.13	0.11	0.10	0.09	0.08
118	0.28	0.24	0.21	0.18	0.17	0.14	0.12	0.10	0.09	0.08
119	0.29	0.25	0.22	0.19	0.17	0.14	0.12	0.11	0.10	0.09
120	0.30	0.26	0.23	0.20	0.18	0.15	0.13	0.11	0.10	0.09
121	0.32	0.27	0.24	0.21	0.19	0.16	0.14	0.12	0.11	0.10
122	0.33	0.28	0.25	0.22	0.20	0.17	0.14	0.12	0.11	0.10
123	0.35	0.30	0.26	0.23	0.21	0.17	0.15	0.13	0.12	0.10
124	0.36	0.31	0.27	0.24	0.22	0.18	0.15	0.13	0.12	0.11
125	0.37	0.32	0.28	0.25	0.22	0.19	0.16	0.14	0.12	0.11
126	0.39	0.33	0.29	0.26	0.23	0.19	0.17	0.14	0.13	0.12
127	0.40	0.34	0.30	0.27	0.24	0.20	0.17	0.15	0.13	0.12
128	0.41	0.35	0.31	0.27	0.25	0.21	0.18	0.15	0.14	0.12
129	0.42	0.36	0.32	0.28	0.25	0.21	0.18	0.16	0.14	0.13
130	0.44	0.37	0.33	0.29	0.26	0.22	0.19	0.16	0.15	0.13
131	0.45	0.39	0.34	0.30	0.27	0.23	0.19	0.17	0.15	0.14
132	0.46	0.40	0.35	0.31	0.28	0.23	0.20	0.17	0.15	0.14
133	0.48	0.41	0.36	0.32	0.29	0.24	0.20	0.18	0.16	0.14
134	0.49	0.42	0.37	0.33	0.29	0.24	0.21	0.18	0.16	0.15
135	0.50	0.43	0.38	0.33	0.30	0.25	0.21	0.19	0.17	0.15
136	0.51	0.44	0.38	0.34	0.31	0.26	0.22	0.19	0.17	0.15
137	0.52	0.45	0.39	0.35	0.31	0.26	0.22	0.20	0.17	0.16
138	0.54	0.46	0.40	0.36	0.32	0.27	0.23	0.20	0.18	0.16
139	0.55	0.47	0.41	0.37	0.33	0.27	0.24	0.21	0.18	0.16
140	0.56	0.48	0.42	0.37	0.34	0.28	0.24	0.21	0.19	0.17
141	0.57	0.49	0.43	0.38	0.34	0.29	0.25	0.21	0.19	0.17
142	0.58	0.50	0.44	0.39	0.35	0.29	0.25	0.22	0.19	0.18
143	0.60	0.51	0.45	0.40	0.36	0.30	0.26	0.22	0.20	0.18
144	0.61	0.52	0.46	0.41	0.36	0.30	0.26	0.23	0.20	0.18
145	0.62	0.53	0.46	0.41	0.37	0.31	0.27	0.23	0.21	0.19
146	0.63	0.54	0.47	0.42	0.38	0.32	0.27	0.24	0.21	0.19
147	0.64	0.55	0.48	0.43	0.39	0.32	0.28	0.24	0.21	0.19
148	0.65	0.56	0.49	0.44	0.39	0.33	0.28	0.25	0.22	0.20
149	0.66	0.57	0.50	0.44	0.40	0.33	0.28	0.25	0.22	0.20
150	0.68	0.58	0.51	0.45	0.41	0.34	0.29	0.25	0.23	0.20

For notes on how to use the table see page 12

TABLE 2. RATES OF GROWTH (COMPOUNDING CONTINUOUSLY)

NUMBER OF PERIODS

FINAL AMOUNT	1	2	3	4	5	6	7	8	9	10
152	41.87	20.94	13.96	10.47	8.37	6.98	5.98	5.23	4.65	4.19
154	43.18	21.59	14.39	10.79	8.64	7.20	6.17	5.40	4.80	4.32
156	44.47	22.23	14.82	11.12	8.89	7.41	6.35	5.56	4.94	4.45
158	45.74	22.87	15.25	11.44	9.15	7.62	6.53	5.72	5.08	4.57
160	47.00	23.50	15.67	11.75	9.40	7.83	6.71	5.88	5.22	4.70
162	48.24	24.12	16.08	12.06	9.65	8.04	6.89	6.03	5.36	4.82
164	49.47	24.73	16.49	12.37	9.89	8.24	7.07	6.18	5.50	4.95
166	50.68	25.34	16.89	12.67	10.14	8.45	7.24	6.34	5.63	5.07
168	51.88	25.94	17.29	12.97	10.38	8.65	7.41	6.48	5.76	5.19
170	53.06	26.53	17.69	13.27	10.61	8.84	7.58	6.63	5.90	5.31
172	54.23	27.12	18.08	13.56	10.85	9.04	7.75	6.78	6.03	5.42
174	55.39	27.69	18.46	13.85	11.08	9.23	7.91	6.92	6.15	5.54
176	56.53	28.27	18.84	14.13	11.31	9.42	8.08	7.07	6.28	5.65
178	57.66	28.83	19.22	14.42	11.53	9.61	8.24	7.21	6.41	5.77
180	58.78	29.39	19.59	14.69	11.76	9.80	8.40	7.35	6.53	5.88
182	59.88	29.94	19.96	14.97	11.98	9.98	8.55	7.49	6.65	5.99
184	60.98	30.49	20.33	15.24	12.20	10.16	8.71	7.62	6.78	6.10
186	62.06	31.03	20.69	15.51	12.41	10.34	8.87	7.76	6.90	6.21
188	63.13	31.56	21.04	15.78	12.63	10.52	9.02	7.89	7.01	6.31
190	64.19	32.09	21.40	16.05	12.84	10.70	9.17	8.02	7.13	6.42
192	65.23	32.62	21.74	16.31	13.05	10.87	9.32	8.15	7.25	6.52
194	66.27	33.13	22.09	16.57	13.25	11.04	9.47	8.28	7.36	6.63
196	67.29	33.65	22.43	16.82	13.46	11.22	9.61	8.41	7.48	6.73
198	68.31	34.15	22.77	17.08	13.66	11.38	9.76	8.54	7.59	6.83
200	69.31	34.66	23.10	17.33	13.86	11.55	9.90	8.66	7.70	6.93
202	70.31	35.15	23.44	17.58	14.06	11.72	10.04	8.79	7.81	7.03
204	71.29	35.65	23.76	17.82	14.26	11.88	10.18	8.91	7.92	7.13
206	72.27	36.14	24.09	18.07	14.45	12.05	10.32	9.03	8.03	7.23
208	73.24	36.62	24.41	18.31	14.65	12.21	10.46	9.15	8.14	7.32
210	74.19	37.10	24.73	18.55	14.84	12.37	10.60	9.27	8.24	7.42
212	75.14	37.57	25.05	18.79	15.03	12.52	10.73	9.39	8.35	7.51
214	76.08	38.04	25.36	19.02	15.22	12.68	10.87	9.51	8.45	7.61
216	77.01	38.51	25.67	19.25	15.40	12.84	11.00	9.63	8.56	7.70
218	77.93	38.97	25.98	19.48	15.59	12.99	11.13	9.74	8.66	7.79
220	78.85	39.42	26.28	19.71	15.77	13.14	11.26	9.86	8.76	7.88
222	79.75	39.88	26.58	19.94	15.95	13.29	11.39	9.97	8.86	7.98
224	80.65	40.32	26.88	20.16	16.13	13.44	11.52	10.08	8.96	8.06
226	81.54	40.77	27.18	20.38	16.31	13.59	11.65	10.19	9.06	8.15
228	82.42	41.21	27.47	20.60	16.48	13.74	11.77	10.30	9.16	8.24
230	83.29	41.65	27.76	20.82	16.66	13.88	11.90	10.41	9.25	8.33
232	84.16	42.08	28.05	21.04	16.83	14.03	12.02	10.52	9.35	8.42
234	85.02	42.51	28.34	21.25	17.00	14.17	12.15	10.63	9.45	8.50
236	85.87	42.93	28.62	21.47	17.17	14.31	12.27	10.73	9.54	8.59
238	86.71	43.36	28.90	21.68	17.34	14.45	12.39	10.84	9.63	8.67
240	87.55	43.77	29.18	21.89	17.51	14.59	12.51	10.94	9.73	8.75
242	88.38	44.19	29.46	22.09	17.68	14.73	12.63	11.05	9.82	8.84
244	89.20	44.60	29.73	22.30	17.84	14.87	12.74	11.15	9.91	8.92
246	90.02	45.01	30.01	22.50	18.00	15.00	12.86	11.25	10.00	9.00
248	90.83	45.41	30.28	22.71	18.17	15.14	12.98	11.35	10.09	9.08
250	91.63	45.81	30.54	22.91	18.33	15.27	13.09	11.45	10.18	9.16

For notes on how to use the table see page 12

TABLE 2.   RATES OF GROWTH   (COMPOUNDING CONTINUOUSLY)

NUMBER OF PERIODS

FINAL AMOUNT	12	14	16	18	20	22	24	26	28	30
152	3.49	2.99	2.62	2.33	2.09	1.90	1.74	1.61	1.50	1.40
154	3.60	3.08	2.70	2.40	2.16	1.96	1.80	1.66	1.54	1.44
156	3.71	3.18	2.78	2.47	2.22	2.02	1.85	1.71	1.59	1.48
158	3.81	3.27	2.86	2.54	2.29	2.08	1.91	1.76	1.63	1.52
160	3.92	3.36	2.94	2.61	2.35	2.14	1.96	1.81	1.68	1.57
162	4.02	3.45	3.02	2.68	2.41	2.19	2.01	1.86	1.72	1.61
164	4.12	3.53	3.09	2.75	2.47	2.25	2.06	1.90	1.77	1.65
166	4.22	3.62	3.17	2.82	2.53	2.30	2.11	1.95	1.81	1.69
168	4.32	3.71	3.24	2.88	2.59	2.36	2.16	2.00	1.85	1.73
170	4.42	3.79	3.32	2.95	2.65	2.41	2.21	2.04	1.90	1.77
172	4.52	3.87	3.39	3.01	2.71	2.47	2.26	2.09	1.94	1.81
174	4.62	3.96	3.46	3.08	2.77	2.52	2.31	2.13	1.98	1.85
176	4.71	4.04	3.53	3.14	2.83	2.57	2.36	2.17	2.02	1.88
178	4.81	4.12	3.60	3.20	2.88	2.62	2.40	2.22	2.06	1.92
180	4.90	4.20	3.67	3.27	2.94	2.67	2.45	2.26	2.10	1.96
182	4.99	4.28	3.74	3.33	2.99	2.72	2.50	2.30	2.14	2.00
184	5.08	4.36	3.81	3.39	3.05	2.77	2.54	2.35	2.18	2.03
186	5.17	4.43	3.88	3.45	3.10	2.82	2.59	2.39	2.22	2.07
188	5.26	4.51	3.95	3.51	3.16	2.87	2.63	2.43	2.25	2.10
190	5.35	4.58	4.01	3.57	3.21	2.92	2.67	2.47	2.29	2.14
192	5.44	4.66	4.08	3.62	3.26	2.97	2.72	2.51	2.33	2.17
194	5.52	4.73	4.14	3.68	3.31	3.01	2.76	2.55	2.37	2.21
196	5.61	4.81	4.21	3.74	3.36	3.06	2.80	2.59	2.40	2.24
198	5.69	4.88	4.27	3.79	3.42	3.10	2.85	2.63	2.44	2.28
200	5.78	4.95	4.33	3.85	3.47	3.15	2.89	2.67	2.48	2.31
202	5.86	5.02	4.39	3.91	3.52	3.20	2.93	2.70	2.51	2.34
204	5.94	5.09	4.46	3.96	3.56	3.24	2.97	2.74	2.55	2.38
206	6.02	5.16	4.52	4.02	3.61	3.29	3.01	2.78	2.58	2.41
208	6.10	5.23	4.58	4.07	3.66	3.33	3.05	2.82	2.62	2.44
210	6.18	5.30	4.64	4.12	3.71	3.37	3.09	2.85	2.65	2.47
212	6.26	5.37	4.70	4.17	3.76	3.42	3.13	2.89	2.68	2.50
214	6.34	5.43	4.76	4.23	3.80	3.46	3.17	2.93	2.72	2.54
216	6.42	5.50	4.81	4.28	3.85	3.50	3.21	2.96	2.75	2.57
218	6.49	5.57	4.87	4.33	3.90	3.54	3.25	3.00	2.78	2.60
220	6.57	5.63	4.93	4.38	3.94	3.58	3.29	3.03	2.82	2.63
222	6.65	5.70	4.98	4.43	3.99	3.63	3.32	3.07	2.85	2.66
224	6.72	5.76	5.04	4.48	4.03	3.67	3.36	3.10	2.88	2.69
226	6.79	5.82	5.10	4.53	4.08	3.71	3.40	3.14	2.91	2.72
228	6.87	5.89	5.15	4.58	4.12	3.75	3.43	3.17	2.94	2.75
230	6.94	5.95	5.21	4.63	4.16	3.79	3.47	3.20	2.97	2.78
232	7.01	6.01	5.26	4.68	4.21	3.83	3.51	3.24	3.01	2.81
234	7.08	6.07	5.31	4.72	4.25	3.86	3.54	3.27	3.04	2.83
236	7.16	6.13	5.37	4.77	4.29	3.90	3.58	3.30	3.07	2.86
238	7.23	6.19	5.42	4.82	4.34	3.94	3.61	3.34	3.10	2.89
240	7.30	6.25	5.47	4.86	4.38	3.98	3.65	3.37	3.13	2.92
242	7.36	6.31	5.52	4.91	4.42	4.02	3.68	3.40	3.16	2.95
244	7.43	6.37	5.57	4.96	4.46	4.05	3.72	3.43	3.19	2.97
246	7.50	6.43	5.63	5.00	4.50	4.09	3.75	3.46	3.21	3.00
248	7.57	6.49	5.68	5.05	4.54	4.13	3.78	3.49	3.24	3.03
250	7.64	6.54	5.73	5.09	4.58	4.16	3.82	3.52	3.27	3.05

For notes on how to use the table see page 12

TABLE 2.   RATES OF GROWTH   (COMPOUNDING CONTINUOUSLY)

NUMBER OF PERIODS

FINAL AMOUNT	32	34	36	38	40	42	44	46	48	50
152	1.31	1.23	1.16	1.10	1.05	1.00	0.95	0.91	0.87	0.84
154	1.35	1.27	1.20	1.14	1.08	1.03	0.98	0.94	0.90	0.86
156	1.39	1.31	1.24	1.17	1.11	1.06	1.01	0.97	0.93	0.89
158	1.43	1.35	1.27	1.20	1.14	1.09	1.04	0.99	0.95	0.91
160	1.47	1.38	1.31	1.24	1.18	1.12	1.07	1.02	0.98	0.94
162	1.51	1.42	1.34	1.27	1.21	1.15	1.10	1.05	1.01	0.96
164	1.55	1.45	1.37	1.30	1.24	1.18	1.12	1.08	1.03	0.99
166	1.58	1.49	1.41	1.33	1.27	1.21	1.15	1.10	1.06	1.01
168	1.62	1.53	1.44	1.37	1.30	1.24	1.18	1.13	1.08	1.04
170	1.66	1.56	1.47	1.40	1.33	1.26	1.21	1.15	1.11	1.06
172	1.69	1.60	1.51	1.43	1.36	1.29	1.23	1.18	1.13	1.08
174	1.73	1.63	1.54	1.46	1.38	1.32	1.26	1.20	1.15	1.11
176	1.77	1.66	1.57	1.49	1.41	1.35	1.28	1.23	1.18	1.13
178	1.80	1.70	1.60	1.52	1.44	1.37	1.31	1.25	1.20	1.15
180	1.84	1.73	1.63	1.55	1.47	1.40	1.34	1.28	1.22	1.18
182	1.87	1.76	1.66	1.58	1.50	1.43	1.36	1.30	1.25	1.20
184	1.91	1.79	1.69	1.60	1.52	1.45	1.39	1.33	1.27	1.22
186	1.94	1.83	1.72	1.63	1.55	1.48	1.41	1.35	1.29	1.24
188	1.97	1.86	1.75	1.66	1.58	1.50	1.43	1.37	1.32	1.26
190	2.01	1.89	1.78	1.69	1.60	1.53	1.46	1.40	1.34	1.28
192	2.04	1.92	1.81	1.72	1.63	1.55	1.48	1.42	1.36	1.30
194	2.07	1.95	1.84	1.74	1.66	1.58	1.51	1.44	1.38	1.33
196	2.10	1.98	1.87	1.77	1.68	1.60	1.53	1.46	1.40	1.35
198	2.13	2.01	1.90	1.80	1.71	1.63	1.55	1.48	1.42	1.37
200	2.17	2.04	1.93	1.82	1.73	1.65	1.58	1.51	1.44	1.39
202	2.20	2.07	1.95	1.85	1.76	1.67	1.60	1.53	1.46	1.41
204	2.23	2.10	1.98	1.88	1.78	1.70	1.62	1.55	1.49	1.43
206	2.26	2.13	2.01	1.90	1.81	1.72	1.64	1.57	1.51	1.45
208	2.29	2.15	2.03	1.93	1.83	1.74	1.66	1.59	1.53	1.46
210	2.32	2.18	2.06	1.95	1.85	1.77	1.69	1.61	1.55	1.48
212	2.35	2.21	2.09	1.98	1.88	1.79	1.71	1.63	1.57	1.50
214	2.38	2.24	2.11	2.00	1.90	1.81	1.73	1.65	1.59	1.52
216	2.41	2.27	2.14	2.03	1.93	1.83	1.75	1.67	1.60	1.54
218	2.44	2.29	2.16	2.05	1.95	1.86	1.77	1.69	1.62	1.56
220	2.46	2.32	2.19	2.07	1.97	1.88	1.79	1.71	1.64	1.58
222	2.49	2.35	2.22	2.10	1.99	1.90	1.81	1.73	1.66	1.60
224	2.52	2.37	2.24	2.12	2.02	1.92	1.83	1.75	1.68	1.61
226	2.55	2.40	2.26	2.15	2.04	1.94	1.85	1.77	1.70	1.63
228	2.58	2.42	2.29	2.17	2.06	1.96	1.87	1.79	1.72	1.65
230	2.60	2.45	2.31	2.19	2.08	1.98	1.89	1.81	1.74	1.67
232	2.63	2.48	2.34	2.21	2.10	2.00	1.91	1.83	1.75	1.68
234	2.66	2.50	2.36	2.24	2.13	2.02	1.93	1.85	1.77	1.70
236	2.68	2.53	2.39	2.26	2.15	2.04	1.95	1.87	1.79	1.72
238	2.71	2.55	2.41	2.28	2.17	2.06	1.97	1.89	1.81	1.73
240	2.74	2.57	2.43	2.30	2.19	2.08	1.99	1.90	1.82	1.75
242	2.76	2.60	2.45	2.33	2.21	2.10	2.01	1.92	1.84	1.77
244	2.79	2.62	2.48	2.35	2.23	2.12	2.03	1.94	1.86	1.78
246	2.81	2.65	2.50	2.37	2.25	2.14	2.05	1.96	1.88	1.80
248	2.84	2.67	2.52	2.39	2.27	2.16	2.06	1.97	1.89	1.82
250	2.86	2.69	2.55	2.41	2.29	2.18	2.08	1.99	1.91	1.83

For notes on how to use the table see page 12

TABLE 2. RATES OF GROWTH (COMPOUNDING CONTINUOUSLY)

NUMBER OF PERIODS

FINAL AMOUNT	60	70	80	90	100	120	140	160	180	200
152	0.70	0.60	0.52	0.47	0.42	0.35	0.30	0.26	0.23	0.21
154	0.72	0.62	0.54	0.48	0.43	0.36	0.31	0.27	0.24	0.22
156	0.74	0.64	0.56	0.49	0.44	0.37	0.32	0.28	0.25	0.22
158	0.76	0.65	0.57	0.51	0.46	0.38	0.33	0.29	0.25	0.23
160	0.78	0.67	0.59	0.52	0.47	0.39	0.34	0.29	0.26	0.24
162	0.80	0.69	0.60	0.54	0.48	0.40	0.34	0.30	0.27	0.24
164	0.82	0.71	0.62	0.55	0.49	0.41	0.35	0.31	0.27	0.25
166	0.84	0.72	0.63	0.56	0.51	0.42	0.36	0.32	0.28	0.25
168	0.86	0.74	0.65	0.58	0.52	0.43	0.37	0.32	0.29	0.26
170	0.88	0.76	0.66	0.59	0.53	0.44	0.38	0.33	0.29	0.27
172	0.90	0.77	0.68	0.60	0.54	0.45	0.39	0.34	0.30	0.27
174	0.92	0.79	0.69	0.62	0.55	0.46	0.40	0.35	0.31	0.28
176	0.94	0.81	0.71	0.63	0.57	0.47	0.40	0.35	0.31	0.28
178	0.96	0.82	0.72	0.64	0.58	0.48	0.41	0.36	0.32	0.29
180	0.98	0.84	0.73	0.65	0.59	0.49	0.42	0.37	0.33	0.29
182	1.00	0.86	0.75	0.67	0.60	0.50	0.43	0.37	0.33	0.30
184	1.02	0.87	0.76	0.68	0.61	0.51	0.44	0.38	0.34	0.30
186	1.03	0.89	0.78	0.69	0.62	0.52	0.44	0.39	0.34	0.31
188	1.05	0.90	0.79	0.70	0.63	0.53	0.45	0.39	0.35	0.32
190	1.07	0.92	0.80	0.71	0.64	0.53	0.46	0.40	0.36	0.32
192	1.09	0.93	0.82	0.72	0.65	0.54	0.47	0.41	0.36	0.33
194	1.10	0.95	0.83	0.74	0.66	0.55	0.47	0.41	0.37	0.33
196	1.12	0.96	0.84	0.75	0.67	0.56	0.48	0.42	0.37	0.34
198	1.14	0.98	0.85	0.76	0.68	0.57	0.49	0.43	0.38	0.34
200	1.16	0.99	0.87	0.77	0.69	0.58	0.50	0.43	0.39	0.35
202	1.17	1.00	0.88	0.78	0.70	0.59	0.50	0.44	0.39	0.35
204	1.19	1.02	0.89	0.79	0.71	0.59	0.51	0.45	0.40	0.36
206	1.20	1.03	0.90	0.80	0.72	0.60	0.52	0.45	0.40	0.36
208	1.22	1.05	0.92	0.81	0.73	0.61	0.52	0.46	0.41	0.37
210	1.24	1.06	0.93	0.82	0.74	0.62	0.53	0.46	0.41	0.37
212	1.25	1.07	0.94	0.83	0.75	0.63	0.54	0.47	0.42	0.38
214	1.27	1.09	0.95	0.85	0.76	0.63	0.54	0.48	0.42	0.38
216	1.28	1.10	0.96	0.86	0.77	0.64	0.55	0.48	0.43	0.39
218	1.30	1.11	0.97	0.87	0.78	0.65	0.56	0.49	0.43	0.39
220	1.31	1.13	0.99	0.88	0.79	0.66	0.56	0.49	0.44	0.39
222	1.33	1.14	1.00	0.89	0.80	0.66	0.57	0.50	0.44	0.40
224	1.34	1.15	1.01	0.90	0.81	0.67	0.58	0.50	0.45	0.40
226	1.36	1.16	1.02	0.91	0.82	0.68	0.58	0.51	0.45	0.41
228	1.37	1.18	1.03	0.92	0.82	0.69	0.59	0.52	0.46	0.41
230	1.39	1.19	1.04	0.93	0.83	0.69	0.59	0.52	0.46	0.42
232	1.40	1.20	1.05	0.94	0.84	0.70	0.60	0.53	0.47	0.42
234	1.42	1.21	1.06	0.94	0.85	0.71	0.61	0.53	0.47	0.43
236	1.43	1.23	1.07	0.95	0.86	0.72	0.61	0.54	0.48	0.43
238	1.45	1.24	1.08	0.96	0.87	0.72	0.62	0.54	0.48	0.43
240	1.46	1.25	1.09	0.97	0.88	0.73	0.63	0.55	0.49	0.44
242	1.47	1.26	1.10	0.98	0.88	0.74	0.63	0.55	0.49	0.44
244	1.49	1.27	1.11	0.99	0.89	0.74	0.64	0.56	0.50	0.45
246	1.50	1.29	1.13	1.00	0.90	0.75	0.64	0.56	0.50	0.45
248	1.51	1.30	1.14	1.01	0.91	0.76	0.65	0.57	0.50	0.45
250	1.53	1.31	1.15	1.02	0.92	0.76	0.65	0.57	0.51	0.46

For notes on how to use the table see page 12

TABLE 2. RATES OF GROWTH (COMPOUNDING CONTINUOUSLY)

NUMBER OF PERIODS

FINAL AMOUNT	1	2	3	4	5	6	7	8	9	10
260	95.55	47.78	31.85	23.89	19.11	15.93	13.65	11.94	10.62	9.56
270	99.33	49.66	33.11	24.83	19.87	16.55	14.19	12.42	11.04	9.93
280		51.48	34.32	25.74	20.59	17.16	14.71	12.87	11.44	10.30
290		53.24	35.49	26.62	21.29	17.75	15.21	13.31	11.83	10.65
300		54.93	36.62	27.47	21.97	18.31	15.69	13.73	12.21	10.99
310		56.57	37.71	28.29	22.63	18.86	16.16	14.14	12.57	11.31
320		58.16	38.77	29.08	23.26	19.39	16.62	14.54	12.92	11.63
330		59.70	39.80	29.85	23.88	19.90	17.06	14.92	13.27	11.94
340		61.19	40.79	30.59	24.48	20.40	17.48	15.30	13.60	12.24
350		62.64	41.76	31.32	25.06	20.88	17.90	15.66	13.92	12.53
360		64.05	42.70	32.02	25.62	21.35	18.30	16.01	14.23	12.81
370		65.42	43.61	32.71	26.17	21.81	18.69	16.35	14.54	13.08
380		66.75	44.50	33.38	26.70	22.25	19.07	16.69	14.83	13.35
390		68.05	45.37	34.02	27.22	22.68	19.44	17.01	15.12	13.61
400		69.31	46.21	34.66	27.73	23.10	19.80	17.33	15.40	13.86
410		70.55	47.03	35.27	28.22	23.52	20.16	17.64	15.68	14.11
420		71.75	47.84	35.88	28.70	23.92	20.50	17.94	15.95	14.35
430		72.93	48.62	36.47	29.17	24.31	20.84	18.23	16.21	14.59
440		74.08	49.39	37.04	29.63	24.69	21.17	18.52	16.46	14.82
450		75.20	50.14	37.60	30.08	25.07	21.49	18.80	16.71	15.04
460		76.30	50.87	38.15	30.52	25.43	21.80	19.08	16.96	15.26
470		77.38	51.59	38.69	30.95	25.79	22.11	19.34	17.20	15.48
480		78.43	52.29	39.22	31.37	26.14	22.41	19.61	17.43	15.69
490		79.46	52.97	39.73	31.78	26.49	22.70	19.87	17.66	15.89
500		80.47	53.65	40.24	32.19	26.82	22.99	20.12	17.88	16.09
600		89.59	59.73	44.79	35.84	29.86	25.60	22.40	19.91	17.92
700		97.30	64.86	48.65	38.92	32.43	27.80	24.32	21.62	19.46
800			69.31	51.99	41.59	34.66	29.71	25.99	23.10	20.79
900			73.24	54.93	43.94	36.62	31.39	27.47	24.41	21.97
1000			76.75	57.56	46.05	38.38	32.89	28.78	25.58	23.03
1200			82.83	62.12	49.70	41.42	35.50	31.06	27.61	24.85
1400			87.97	65.98	52.78	43.98	37.70	32.99	29.32	26.39
1600			92.42	69.31	55.45	46.21	39.61	34.66	30.81	27.73
1800			96.35	72.26	57.81	48.17	41.29	36.13	32.12	28.90
2000			99.86	74.89	59.91	49.93	42.80	37.45	33.29	29.96
2200				77.28	61.82	51.52	44.16	38.64	34.34	30.91
2400				79.45	63.56	52.97	45.40	39.73	35.31	31.78
2600				81.45	65.16	54.30	46.54	40.73	36.20	32.58
2800				83.31	66.64	55.54	47.60	41.65	37.02	33.32
3000				85.03	68.02	56.69	48.59	42.51	37.79	34.01
3200				86.64	69.31	57.70	49.51	43.32	38.51	34.66
3400				88.16	70.53	58.77	50.38	44.08	39.18	35.26
3600				89.59	71.67	59.73	51.19	44.79	39.82	35.84
3800				90.94	72.75	60.63	51.97	45.47	40.42	36.38
4000				92.22	73.78	61.48	52.70	46.11	40.99	36.89
4200				93.44	74.75	62.29	53.40	46.72	41.53	37.38
4400				94.60	75.68	63.07	54.06	47.30	42.05	37.84
4600				95.72	76.57	63.81	54.69	47.86	42.54	38.29
4800				96.78	77.42	64.52	55.30	48.39	43.01	38.71
5000				97.80	78.24	65.20	55.89	48.90	43.47	39.12

For notes on how to use the table see page 12

TABLE 2.   RATES OF GROWTH   (COMPOUNDING CONTINUOUSLY)

NUMBER OF PERIODS

FINAL AMOUNT	12	14	16	18	20	22	24	26	28	30
260	7.96	6.83	5.97	5.31	4.78	4.34	3.98	3.68	3.41	3.19
270	8.28	7.09	6.21	5.52	4.97	4.51	4.14	3.82	3.55	3.31
280	8.58	7.35	6.44	5.72	5.15	4.68	4.29	3.96	3.68	3.43
290	8.87	7.61	6.65	5.92	5.32	4.84	4.44	4.10	3.80	3.55
300	9.16	7.85	6.87	6.10	5.49	4.99	4.58	4.23	3.92	3.66
310	9.43	8.08	7.07	6.29	5.66	5.14	4.71	4.35	4.04	3.77
320	9.69	8.31	7.27	6.46	5.82	5.29	4.85	4.47	4.15	3.88
330	9.95	8.53	7.46	6.63	5.97	5.43	4.97	4.59	4.26	3.98
340	10.20	8.74	7.65	6.80	6.12	5.56	5.10	4.71	4.37	4.08
350	10.44	8.95	7.83	6.96	6.26	5.69	5.22	4.82	4.47	4.18
360	10.67	9.15	8.01	7.12	6.40	5.82	5.34	4.93	4.57	4.27
370	10.90	9.35	8.18	7.27	6.54	5.95	5.45	5.03	4.67	4.36
380	11.13	9.54	8.34	7.42	6.68	6.07	5.56	5.13	4.77	4.45
390	11.34	9.72	8.51	7.56	6.80	6.19	5.67	5.23	4.86	4.54
400	11.55	9.90	8.66	7.70	6.93	6.30	5.78	5.33	4.95	4.62
410	11.76	10.08	8.82	7.84	7.05	6.41	5.88	5.43	5.04	4.70
420	11.96	10.25	8.97	7.97	7.18	6.52	5.98	5.52	5.13	4.78
430	12.16	10.42	9.12	8.10	7.29	6.63	6.08	5.61	5.21	4.86
440	12.35	10.58	9.26	8.23	7.41	6.73	6.17	5.70	5.29	4.94
450	12.53	10.74	9.40	8.36	7.52	6.84	6.27	5.78	5.37	5.01
460	12.72	10.90	9.54	8.48	7.63	6.94	6.36	5.87	5.45	5.09
470	12.90	11.05	9.67	8.60	7.74	7.03	6.45	5.95	5.53	5.16
480	13.07	11.20	9.80	8.71	7.84	7.13	6.54	6.03	5.60	5.23
490	13.24	11.35	9.93	8.83	7.95	7.22	6.62	6.11	5.68	5.30
500	13.41	11.50	10.06	8.94	8.05	7.32	6.71	6.19	5.75	5.36
600	14.93	12.80	11.20	9.95	8.96	8.14	7.47	6.89	6.40	5.97
700	16.22	13.90	12.16	10.81	9.73	8.85	8.11	7.48	6.95	6.49
800	17.33	14.85	13.00	11.55	10.40	9.45	8.66	8.00	7.43	6.93
900	18.31	15.69	13.73	12.21	10.99	9.99	9.16	8.45	7.85	7.32
1000	19.19	16.45	14.39	12.79	11.51	10.47	9.59	8.86	8.22	7.68
1200	20.71	17.75	15.53	13.81	12.42	11.30	10.35	9.56	8.87	8.28
1400	21.99	18.85	16.49	14.66	13.20	12.00	11.00	10.15	9.43	8.80
1600	23.10	19.80	17.33	15.40	13.86	12.60	11.55	10.66	9.90	9.24
1800	24.09	20.65	18.06	16.06	14.45	13.14	12.04	11.12	10.32	9.63
2000	24.96	21.40	18.72	16.64	14.98	13.62	12.48	11.52	10.70	9.99
2200	25.76	22.08	19.32	17.17	15.46	14.05	12.88	11.89	11.04	10.30
2400	26.48	22.70	19.86	17.66	15.89	14.45	13.24	12.22	11.35	10.59
2600	27.15	23.27	20.36	18.10	16.29	14.81	13.58	12.53	11.64	10.86
2800	27.77	23.80	20.83	18.51	16.66	15.15	13.88	12.82	11.90	11.11
3000	28.34	24.29	21.26	18.90	17.01	15.46	14.17	13.08	12.15	11.34
3200	28.88	24.76	21.66	19.25	17.33	15.75	14.44	13.33	12.38	11.55
3400	29.39	25.19	22.04	19.59	17.63	16.03	14.69	13.56	12.59	11.75
3600	29.86	25.60	22.40	19.91	17.92	16.29	14.93	13.78	12.80	11.95
3800	30.31	25.98	22.73	20.21	18.19	16.53	15.16	13.99	12.99	12.13
4000	30.74	26.35	23.06	20.49	18.44	16.77	15.37	14.19	13.17	12.30
4200	31.15	26.70	23.36	20.76	18.69	16.99	15.57	14.38	13.35	12.46
4400	31.53	27.03	23.65	21.02	18.92	17.20	15.77	14.55	13.51	12.61
4600	31.91	27.35	23.93	21.27	19.14	17.40	15.95	14.73	13.67	12.76
4800	32.26	27.65	24.20	21.51	19.36	17.60	16.13	14.89	13.83	12.90
5000	32.60	27.94	24.45	21.73	19.56	17.78	16.30	15.05	13.97	13.04

For notes on how to use the table see page 12

TABLE 2. RATES OF GROWTH (COMPOUNDING CONTINUOUSLY)

NUMBER OF PERIODS

FINAL AMOUNT	32	34	36	38	40	42	44	46	48	50
260	2.99	2.81	2.65	2.51	2.39	2.28	2.17	2.08	1.99	1.91
270	3.10	2.92	2.76	2.61	2.48	2.36	2.26	2.16	2.07	1.99
280	3.22	3.03	2.86	2.71	2.57	2.45	2.34	2.24	2.15	2.06
290	3.33	3.13	2.96	2.80	2.66	2.54	2.42	2.31	2.22	2.13
300	3.43	3.23	3.05	2.89	2.75	2.62	2.50	2.39	2.29	2.20
310	3.54	3.33	3.14	2.98	2.83	2.69	2.57	2.46	2.36	2.26
320	3.63	3.42	3.23	3.06	2.91	2.77	2.64	2.53	2.42	2.33
330	3.73	3.51	3.32	3.14	2.98	2.84	2.71	2.60	2.49	2.39
340	3.82	3.60	3.40	3.22	3.06	2.91	2.78	2.66	2.55	2.45
350	3.91	3.68	3.48	3.30	3.13	2.98	2.85	2.72	2.61	2.51
360	4.00	3.77	3.56	3.37	3.20	3.05	2.91	2.78	2.67	2.56
370	4.09	3.85	3.63	3.44	3.27	3.12	2.97	2.84	2.73	2.62
380	4.17	3.93	3.71	3.51	3.34	3.18	3.03	2.90	2.78	2.67
390	4.25	4.00	3.78	3.58	3.40	3.24	3.09	2.96	2.84	2.72
400	4.33	4.08	3.85	3.65	3.47	3.30	3.15	3.01	2.89	2.77
410	4.41	4.15	3.92	3.71	3.53	3.36	3.21	3.07	2.94	2.82
420	4.48	4.22	3.99	3.78	3.59	3.42	3.26	3.12	2.99	2.87
430	4.56	4.29	4.05	3.84	3.65	3.47	3.32	3.17	3.04	2.92
440	4.63	4.36	4.12	3.90	3.70	3.53	3.37	3.22	3.09	2.96
450	4.70	4.42	4.18	3.96	3.76	3.58	3.42	3.27	3.13	3.01
460	4.77	4.49	4.24	4.02	3.82	3.63	3.47	3.32	3.18	3.05
470	4.84	4.55	4.30	4.07	3.87	3.68	3.52	3.36	3.22	3.10
480	4.90	4.61	4.36	4.13	3.92	3.73	3.57	3.41	3.27	3.14
490	4.97	4.67	4.41	4.18	3.97	3.78	3.61	3.45	3.31	3.18
500	5.03	4.73	4.47	4.24	4.02	3.83	3.66	3.50	3.35	3.22
600	5.60	5.27	4.98	4.72	4.48	4.27	4.07	3.90	3.73	3.58
700	6.08	5.72	5.41	5.12	4.86	4.63	4.42	4.23	4.05	3.89
800	6.50	6.12	5.78	5.47	5.20	4.95	4.73	4.52	4.33	4.16
900	6.87	6.46	6.10	5.78	5.49	5.23	4.99	4.78	4.58	4.39
1000	7.20	6.77	6.40	6.06	5.76	5.48	5.23	5.01	4.80	4.61
1200	7.77	7.31	6.90	6.54	6.21	5.92	5.65	5.40	5.18	4.97
1400	8.25	7.76	7.33	6.94	6.60	6.28	6.00	5.74	5.50	5.28
1600	8.66	8.15	7.70	7.30	6.93	6.60	6.30	6.03	5.78	5.55
1800	9.03	8.50	8.03	7.61	7.23	6.88	6.57	6.28	6.02	5.78
2000	9.36	8.81	8.32	7.88	7.49	7.13	6.81	6.51	6.24	5.99
2200	9.66	9.09	8.59	8.13	7.73	7.36	7.03	6.72	6.44	6.18
2400	9.93	9.35	8.83	8.36	7.95	7.57	7.22	6.91	6.62	6.36
2600	10.18	9.58	9.05	8.57	8.15	7.76	7.40	7.08	6.79	6.52
2800	10.41	9.80	9.26	8.77	8.33	7.93	7.57	7.24	6.94	6.66
3000	10.63	10.00	9.45	8.95	8.50	8.10	7.73	7.39	7.09	6.80
3200	10.83	10.19	9.63	9.12	8.66	8.25	7.88	7.53	7.22	6.93
3400	11.02	10.37	9.80	9.28	8.82	8.40	8.01	7.67	7.35	7.05
3600	11.20	10.54	9.95	9.43	8.96	8.53	8.14	7.79	7.47	7.17
3800	11.37	10.70	10.10	9.57	9.09	8.66	8.27	7.91	7.58	7.28
4000	11.53	10.85	10.25	9.71	9.22	8.78	8.38	8.02	7.69	7.38
4200	11.68	10.99	10.38	9.84	9.34	8.90	8.49	8.13	7.79	7.48
4400	11.83	11.13	10.51	9.96	9.46	9.01	8.60	8.23	7.88	7.57
4600	11.96	11.26	10.64	10.08	9.57	9.12	8.70	8.32	7.98	7.66
4800	12.10	11.39	10.75	10.19	9.68	9.22	8.80	8.42	8.07	7.74
5000	12.23	11.51	10.87	10.29	9.78	9.31	8.89	8.50	8.15	7.82

For notes on how to use the table see page 12

TABLE 2. RATES OF GROWTH (COMPOUNDING CONTINUOUSLY)

NUMBER OF PERIODS

FINAL AMOUNT	60	70	80	90	100	120	140	160	180	200
260	1.59	1.37	1.19	1.06	0.96	0.80	0.68	0.60	0.53	0.48
270	1.66	1.42	1.24	1.10	0.99	0.83	0.71	0.62	0.55	0.50
280	1.72	1.47	1.29	1.14	1.03	0.86	0.74	0.64	0.57	0.51
290	1.77	1.52	1.33	1.18	1.06	0.89	0.76	0.67	0.59	0.53
300	1.83	1.57	1.37	1.22	1.10	0.92	0.78	0.69	0.61	0.55
310	1.89	1.62	1.41	1.26	1.13	0.94	0.81	0.71	0.63	0.57
320	1.94	1.66	1.45	1.29	1.16	0.97	0.83	0.73	0.65	0.58
330	1.99	1.71	1.49	1.33	1.19	0.99	0.85	0.75	0.66	0.60
340	2.04	1.75	1.53	1.36	1.22	1.02	0.87	0.76	0.68	0.61
350	2.09	1.79	1.57	1.39	1.25	1.04	0.89	0.78	0.70	0.63
360	2.13	1.83	1.60	1.42	1.28	1.07	0.91	0.80	0.71	0.64
370	2.18	1.87	1.64	1.45	1.31	1.09	0.93	0.82	0.73	0.65
380	2.23	1.91	1.67	1.48	1.34	1.11	0.95	0.83	0.74	0.67
390	2.27	1.94	1.70	1.51	1.36	1.13	0.97	0.85	0.76	0.68
400	2.31	1.98	1.73	1.54	1.39	1.16	0.99	0.87	0.77	0.69
410	2.35	2.02	1.76	1.57	1.41	1.18	1.01	0.88	0.78	0.71
420	2.39	2.05	1.79	1.59	1.44	1.20	1.03	0.90	0.80	0.72
430	2.43	2.08	1.82	1.62	1.46	1.22	1.04	0.91	0.81	0.73
440	2.47	2.12	1.85	1.65	1.48	1.23	1.06	0.93	0.82	0.74
450	2.51	2.15	1.88	1.67	1.50	1.25	1.07	0.94	0.84	0.75
460	2.54	2.18	1.91	1.70	1.53	1.27	1.09	0.95	0.85	0.76
470	2.58	2.21	1.93	1.72	1.55	1.29	1.11	0.97	0.86	0.77
480	2.61	2.24	1.96	1.74	1.57	1.31	1.12	0.98	0.87	0.78
490	2.65	2.27	1.99	1.77	1.59	1.32	1.14	0.99	0.88	0.79
500	2.68	2.30	2.01	1.79	1.61	1.34	1.15	1.01	0.89	0.80
600	2.99	2.56	2.24	1.99	1.79	1.49	1.28	1.12	1.00	0.90
700	3.24	2.78	2.43	2.16	1.95	1.62	1.39	1.22	1.08	0.97
800	3.47	2.97	2.60	2.31	2.08	1.73	1.49	1.30	1.16	1.04
900	3.66	3.14	2.75	2.44	2.20	1.83	1.57	1.37	1.22	1.10
1000	3.84	3.29	2.88	2.56	2.30	1.92	1.64	1.44	1.28	1.15
1200	4.14	3.55	3.11	2.76	2.48	2.07	1.77	1.55	1.38	1.24
1400	4.40	3.77	3.30	2.93	2.64	2.20	1.89	1.65	1.47	1.32
1600	4.62	3.96	3.47	3.08	2.77	2.31	1.98	1.73	1.54	1.39
1800	4.82	4.13	3.61	3.21	2.89	2.41	2.06	1.81	1.61	1.45
2000	4.99	4.28	3.74	3.33	3.00	2.50	2.14	1.87	1.66	1.50
2200	5.15	4.42	3.86	3.43	3.09	2.58	2.21	1.93	1.72	1.55
2400	5.30	4.54	3.97	3.53	3.18	2.65	2.27	1.99	1.77	1.59
2600	5.43	4.65	4.07	3.62	3.26	2.72	2.33	2.04	1.81	1.63
2800	5.55	4.76	4.17	3.70	3.33	2.78	2.38	2.08	1.85	1.67
3000	5.67	4.86	4.25	3.78	3.40	2.83	2.43	2.13	1.89	1.70
3200	5.78	4.95	4.33	3.85	3.47	2.89	2.48	2.17	1.93	1.73
3400	5.88	5.04	4.41	3.92	3.53	2.94	2.52	2.20	1.96	1.76
3600	5.97	5.12	4.48	3.98	3.58	2.99	2.56	2.24	1.99	1.79
3800	6.06	5.20	4.55	4.04	3.64	3.03	2.60	2.27	2.02	1.82
4000	6.15	5.27	4.61	4.10	3.69	3.07	2.63	2.31	2.05	1.84
4200	6.23	5.34	4.67	4.15	3.74	3.11	2.67	2.34	2.08	1.87
4400	6.31	5.41	4.73	4.20	3.78	3.15	2.70	2.37	2.10	1.89
4600	6.38	5.47	4.79	4.25	3.83	3.19	2.73	2.39	2.13	1.91
4800	6.45	5.53	4.84	4.30	3.87	3.23	2.77	2.42	2.15	1.94
5000	6.52	5.59	4.89	4.35	3.91	3.26	2.79	2.45	2.17	1.96

For notes on how to use the table see page 12

UNIVERSITY OF CAMBRIDGE

DEPARTMENT OF APPLIED ECONOMICS

Occasional Papers

1 White-Collar Redundancy: A Case Study

By Dorothy Wedderburn

Mrs Wedderburn's case study is that of the dismissals which followed the cancellation of the defence contract for the Blue Water Guided Missile at the Luton and Stevenage factories of English Electric Aviation Ltd.

She first describes how the management dealt with the problem of bringing about a sharp and large reduction in the labour force, and then investigates what were the experiences and attitudes of the dismissed men, how long it took them to find jobs and what sort of jobs they found. It concludes with a brief discussion of possible lessons to be learned from the experience.

2 Railway Workshops: The Problems of Contraction

By P. Lesley Cook

In September 1962 a major plan for the contraction and reorganization of the main workshops of British Railways was announced. This plan proposed a reduction in the staff from 62,000 to 40,000 by 1967, the closure of a number of the large workshops and considerable investment in modern layouts. Dr Cook was given special facilities to make an independent investigation of the factors which made such a plan necessary and the basis for the numerous decisions.

The problems of contraction when combined with reorganization and investment are complicated and present unfamiliar theoretical problems, particularly in connexion with the utilization of capacity, the timing of action and the length of the time horizon which must be considered. The problems are not peculiar to the railway workshops and much of the discussion is of general application. The planning involved difficult choices as to which works should be retained and which men made redundant; the whole question of the social responsibilities of industry for easing the hardships of unemployment and redundancy is raised in an acute form. The conflicts between social responsibilities towards individuals and localities and the objective of efficiency and low costs had to be resolved.

3 Economies of Large-scale Production in British Industry

An Introductory Study

By C. F. Pratten and R. M. Dean, in collaboration with Audrey Silberston

The Department of Applied Economics is engaged on a wide-ranging study of the economies of large-scale production in selected British industries. Studies of four industries have already been made and are described in this occasional paper, which is in the nature of a progress report. The four industries are book-printing, footwear manufacture, oil refining and the steel industry. The paper contains an introductory chapter which describes the different forms which 'large-scale production' may take (e.g. large factories or long runs); the methods and difficulties of measuring economies of scale are also discussed and attention is drawn to the different approaches used in the past.

The study should interest not only those with a particular interest in these four industries but also all those concerned with the efficient organization of British industry. It should also be useful for students taking courses in industrial organization.

4 Redundancy and the Railwaymen

By Dorothy Wedderburn

This is a study of the social consequences of the closure of railway workshops. Two workshops were selected for study, one at Gorton, Manchester—an area of relatively high employment—and one at Faverdale, Darlington—already scheduled as a Development District and with more workshop closures to come. Mrs Wedderburn describes how the workers dismissed—men with specialised skills, with long service in the workshop, whose fathers before them were often railwaymen—set about the task of finding new jobs. She and her team investigate how quickly the men found jobs, what sort of jobs they were and whether they had to move to find work; the crucial importance of the nation-wide economic expansion in 1964 becomes vividly apparent, as do the special problems of the men over sixty and others who have physical disabilities. They also investigate how the men adjusted socially, psychologically and economically to the change, and how far the arrangements made by the British Railways Board for handling the redundancy facilitated the change for the men.

This paper—which is a sequel to Mrs Wedderburn's earlier study White Collar Redundancy—should be of great value to Ministers and officials, business men and trade union leaders, students of economics and sociology, and indeed all who are concerned with one of today's leading problems.

5 Parking Space for Cars: Assessing the Demand

By C. J. Roth

Many city authorities are faced with two urgent and related problems: how many parking-spaces to provide, and what to charge for them.

In this paper Mr Roth reports on three pioneer attempts by the Department of Applied Economics, Cambridge, to assess the demand for parking space at various price-levels, made in the towns of Cambridge, Luton and Liverpool respectively. The account reveals many of the problems inherent in making the necessary surveys and analysing the results: it concludes that a combination of methods is needed to give the best guidance.

Some of the interesting quantitative conclusions concern the amount of potential demand which is now "frustrated" (because motorists do not take their cars into the city for fear of difficulty in finding a parking space), and the extent to which various levels of parking charge affect the demand.

This paper should be of great value to all who are concerned about parking problems, and more especially to those who have to make quantitative decisions about the facilities to be provided and the prices to be charged. No amount of data about the consequences of different policies can, of itself, answer the political questions involved, but without the data, no rational decisions can be taken.

6 Wage Trends, Wage Policies and Collective Bargaining the Problems for Underdeveloped Countries

By H. A. Turner

This paper is based on Professor Turner's experience over a period of some five years as a consultant to the Governments of various underdeveloped countries or to the International Labour Organisation. It considers how far the problems of wage-fixation in under-developed countries are or are not similar to those in advanced countries, and what the implications are for policy-making bodies.